PRAISE FOR *Nikolai and the Others*

"I would want [*Nikolai and the Others*] to be seen by anyone interested in Balanchine and his choreography. . . . The research done by Mr. Nelson is exceptional. . . . The world of Russian émigrés is Chekhovian in both intimacy and intricacy."
—ALASTAIR MACAULAY, Chief Dance Critic, *The New York Times*

"Mr. Nelson paints a group portrait of artists for whom time is forever out of joint. . . . [*Nikolai and the Others*] summons both a sense of place and displacement with such naturalness that you forget that you're watching titans at play. . . . Mr. Nelson is always an emphatic chronicler of human frailty, waywardness and even cruelty."
—BEN BRANTLEY, *The New York Times*

"An engrossing work that transports Chekhov to the threshold of the Cold War. The country house isn't in the Russian provinces but in Westport, Connecticut, and it's 1948. The characters are exiles whose childhoods on large estates ended with the czar's rule, decades earlier. . . . Though they talk a lot, they don't just talk; they are managing, midwifing, or directly making some of the twentieth century's greatest art. . . . *Nikolai and the Others* makes the unmistakable point that artistic freedom is not always conducive to art and, in any case, is never free."
—JESSE GREEN, *New York*

"I felt as if I had just experienced a beautifully detailed novel about some fascinating historic figures."
—ROMA TORRE, *NY1*

"Richard Nelson's inspired new play, *Nikolai and the Others*, bristles with compelling ideas and complex characters in equal measure. . . . Rich in emotional detail and in its evocation of an era in culture deserving examination and interpretation."
—JEREMY GERARD, *Bloomberg*

"Nelson has created a beautifully mo[...]
America. [And he] skillfully encapsula[...]
émigrés' lives as they struggle with art[...]
past loves, yearning for their long-los[...]
political issues."
—JENNI[...]

RICHARD NELSON's plays include *The Apple Family* plays for the Public Theater, *Farewell to the Theatre*, *Frank's Home*, *Conversations in Tusculum*, *Rodney's Wife*, *Franny's Way*, *Madame Melville*, *Goodnight Children Everywhere*, *New England*, *Two Shakespearean Actors*, and *Some Americans Abroad*. He wrote the screenplays for *Hyde Park on Hudson* and *Ethan Frome*, and the books for the musicals *James Joyce's The Dead* and *My Life With Albertine*. He is the recipient of numerous awards, including an Olivier for Best Play, a Tony, the PEN/Laura Pels Master Playwright Award, and an Academy Award from the American Academy of Arts and Letters. He is an Honorary Associate Artist of The Royal Shakespeare Company. He lives in Rhinebeck, New York.

Nikolai and the Others

Nikolai and the Others

A PLAY BY

RICHARD NELSON

Preface by André Bishop

OVERLOOK DUCKWORTH
New York • London

This edition first published in the United States and the United Kingdom
in 2013 by Overlook Duckworth, Peter Mayer Publishers, Inc.

NEW YORK
141 Wooster Street
New York, NY 10012
www.overlookpress.com
For bulk and special sales, please contact sales@overlookny.com,
or write us at above address.

LONDON
30 Calvin Street
London E1 6NW
info@duckworth-publishers.co.uk
www.ducknet.co.uk
For bulk and special sales, please contact sales@duckworth-publishers.co.uk,
or write us at the above address.

Cataloging-in-Publication Data is available from the Library of Congress.
A catalogue record for this book is available from the British Library.

Book design and type formatting by Bernard Schleifer
Manufactured in the United States of America
ISBN 978-1-4683-0853-2 (US)
ISBN 978-0-7156-4748-6 (UK)
1 3 5 7 9 10 8 6 4 2

For Patrick Herold

I am not trying to prove anything. That is, trying to prove something quite other than the fact of dancing.

—GEORGE BALANCHINE

Preface

Richard Nelson came to see me a few years ago with a good idea. Would Lincoln Center Theater be interested in commissioning a play about Balanchine and Stravinsky in America, the creation of the ballet *Orpheus*, and the beginning of the cultural cold war between the United States and Russia? To do such a play at Lincoln Center, the home of the New York City Ballet, and a cultural icon, would be so appropriate. *When do we start?* was some version of my response! Armed with various books about ballet, Nicholas Nabokov, the impact of the CIA on the arts, Lincoln Center Theater set about preparing for this tantalizing prospect.

We are currently living in a golden age of American playwriting though we may not realize it or even want to admit it. New plays of distinction and range are being produced all over the United States, and we now have many generations of playwrights, actively working, actively being produced. Richard Nelson, to my mind, really heads the pack and has for years, with an astounding body of work that covers the widest possible spectrum of human activity—his plays are historical, intellectual, lyrical, personal, familial, comical, tragical (I sound like Polonius!), and he works as a translator and adaptor, screenwriter, and director, and teacher. He has many theories about writing, about acting, about design and he presents these theories with conviction and clarity. He has been doing this for over thirty years, and has never run out of stories or of new ideas. Is it possible to be this wide-ranging and yet always be distinctively Nelsonian? Yes!

Nikolai and the Others is one of several plays Richard has written about American artists—in this case Russian artists attempting to become American artists. The play, which unfolds rather like a Russian novel, shows us a day in the life of some notably great artists and asks that we be alert observers and watch these émigré artists and their friends live out their lives during a weekend on a farm in Westport, Connecticut.

They laugh, they cry, they eat (oh, how they eat!), they live their lives of exile, and two of them—Balanchine and Stravinsky—create a new ballet. The play is about friendship, about living in a new culture and wanting to assimilate, about those who have talent and those who don't, and most of all, the play is about art, the lasting power of art and the supreme importance of artists and those who care for them.

This is one of those pebble in a pond plays, by which I mean that reading the play is like throwing a pebble into a pond, making ever wider and expanding circles from the center. There is simply so much richness, so many layers, so much *life*.

I used to tell friends coming to see *Nikolai and the Others* that this was not a play (or a production) that would come out to you, desperate to please: you, the audience, had to surrender and come to *it*.

If the text evokes a whole world as I suggest, the production, beautifully directed by David Cromer, created a whole world, and featured a stunning ensemble of distinguished and committed actors.

We had originally commissioned the play for the 1000-seat Beaumont Theater, but after an onstage reading it became clear that the play, despite its enormous cast and multiple sets, needed an intimate space where nothing need be pushed, where actors could simply "be" without forcing, where the audience would feel like flies on the wall and not spectators at a ballgame. David Cromer brought wondrously varied staging and a real sense of the life of a house. His vision produced a play filled with real people, with a design that was rustic and gritty and not "typical genteel country house" design, with a cast of actors who would sound unaffected and not play "artists," and an actor who would *really* play the piano during the ballet rehearsals. Difficult to be sure, but it all paid off because it was always in support of Richard's text.

We were greatly helped by the New York City Ballet who coached our dancers and talked to our cast and were genuinely enthusiastic; we had feared they might be suspicious about what these theater people across the Lincoln Center plaza were up to with their beloved Balanchine and his great ballet *Orpheus*. They turned out to be generous colleagues.

So a project that began as a gleam in a gifted playwright's eye became, after a few years, a vivid and special dramatic event. Night after night our audiences were filled with actors and dancers who rejoiced to see a play that spoke to them so vividly.

Any play that contains this speech is destined to live forever:

> Strip away everything else from a person, and art is what you have left. Some people call this the soul. But I know it as art. Art: our record that we have lived, the breath that gives us life. They can take away our homes and countries, our families, take away our money and beliefs and hopes; Make us compromise and turn us into creatures we do not recognize. Creatures we might even despise. They can do all that—and then what is left of us—is art. There to remind us that we are human beings. It is not some super-natural gift of the gods, but the most human of human acts. Like eating, like sex, or love, like laughter, like the warmth one feels for family and friends. It is who and what we all are. And it is how we know about ourselves.

There wasn't a dry eye, let me tell you. I salute Richard Nelson for his extraordinary play, a model of research, intelligence, and passion.

—ANDRÉ BISHOP
Lincoln Center Theater
August 2013

Nikolai and the Others received its commission and world premiere at Lincoln Center Theater with previews beginning on April 4, 2013, and opening on May 6, 2013. André Bishop, Artistic Director; Bernard Gersten, Executive Producer; Adam Siegel, Managing Director. The production was directed by David Cromer. Scenic design by Marsha Ginsberg; costume design by Jane Greenwood; lighting design by Ken Billington; sound design by Daniel Kluger; choreography by George Balanchine; ballet staging by Rosemary Dunleavy; Ballet Master Jeff Edwards; Stage Manager Richard Hodge; and Press Agent Philip Rinaldi at Philip Rinaldi Publicity.

CAST

BETSY AIDEM	Lisa Sokoloff
NATALIA ALONSO	Maria Tallchief
BLAIR BROWN	Vera Stravinsky
MICHAEL CERVERIS	George Balanchine
ANTHONY COCHRANE	Aleksi Karpov
LAUREN CULPEPPER	Anna
ALVIN EPSTEIN	Sergey Sudeikin
KATHRYN ERBE	Natasha Nabokov
JOHN GLOVER	Igor Stravinsky
JENNIFER GRACE	Natalia
KATIE KREISLER	Evgenia
STEPHEN KUNKEN	Nikolai Nabokov
HAVILAND MORRIS	Lucia Davidova
DALE PLACE	Serge Koussevitzky
JOHN PROCACCINO	Vladimir Sokoloff
MICHAEL ROSEN	Nicholas Magallanes
GARETH SAXE	Charles Bohlen
ALAN SCHMUCKLER	Kolya Sudeikin

Characters

THE RUSSIANS:

The Men.

NIKOLAI "NICKY" DIMITRIEVICH NABOKOV, 40s, a Composer
SERGE KOUSSEVITZKY, 72, a Conductor
GEORGE BALANCHINE, 42, a Choreographer
IGOR STRAVINSKY, 64, a Composer
SERGEY SUDEIKIN, 66, a Painter and Set Designer, and
    ex-husband of Vera Stravinsky
KOLYA SUDEIKIN, 30s, George's rehearsal Pianist and Sergey's
    nephew
ALEKSI KARPOV, 64, a piano teacher, engaged to Natasha
VLADIMIR SOKOLOFF, 50s, a film and stage Actor, married to Lisa

The Women.

VERA STRAVINSKY, 60, Igor's wife, a former costume designer,
    ex-wife of Sudeikin
LUCIA DAVIDOVA, 40s, the weekend's hostess, George's
    confidant
NATASHA NABOKOV, 40s, Nikolai's first wife, George's other confidant,
    engaged to Karpov
ANNA, 19, Lucia's niece, studying to be a dancer
EVGENIA, 39, runs the School of Ballet
NATALIA, 35, works for Evgenia at the School of Ballet
LISA SOKOLOFF, 50s, Vladimir's wife, and Vera Stravinsky's
    best friend

THE AMERICANS:

MARIA TALLCHIEF, 23, Dancer and married to George Balanchine
NICHOLAS MAGALLANES, 26, Dancer
CHARLES "CHIP" BOHLEN, 42, State Department Official, and fluent
    Russian-speaker

Time and Place

The play takes place over a weekend on a farm outside Westport, Connecticut, in the spring of 1948.

[NOTE: For nearly all of the play the characters speak Russian. When they speak Russian, they do not speak with an accent. When the Russian characters speak English, they speak with an accent—these lines are in _underscored italics_.]

Scene One

The porch of LUCIA DAVIDOVA's *country house, in the woods, outside Westport, Connecticut, spring, 1948.*

Wicker chairs, tables—we could be in Russia, circa 1905. Piano music—fragments, often repeated—comes from the study, inside the house. Afternoon.

NICKY *sits in a chair, waiting, paying some attention to the music being played off.*

Pause.

VERA STRAVINSKY (60) *enters from the house. She sits, picking up embroidery that she had left on the chair.*

VERA (as she sits)

Nikolai Dimitrievich, I told Natasha you were here. She'll be right out.

(new thought, as she embroiders)

She's looking very nice.

NICKY

She always does.

Music off catches his attention, then:

We run into each other. From time to time.

Short pause.

VERA

And you are still divorced.

NICKY

I am.

VERA (embroidering)

That's how many divorces?

NICKY

Two. Still only two.

Smiles.

VERA (*embroidering*)

Natasha and . . . ?

NICKY

The—"one who wasn't Russian."

NATASHA (*early 40s*) [NICKY'*s first wife*] *enters from the house, she is cleaning her hands on her apron as she approaches* NICKY.

NICKY *stands and they greet.*

VERA

Natasha and I were talking before you arrived about ex-husbands.

NICKY

Were you.

NATASHA

Mostly about Sergey, Nicky. Vera's excited about seeing Sergey.
She smiles.

NICKY

I happened to see him last week. I was shocked. The weight he's lost.

NATASHA

Nicky . . .

VERA

How much weight? I haven't seen Sergey for at least a year.
She looks to them and gets no response.
I want to be prepared.
She buries herself in her embroidering as:
In Petersburg he'd like to walk around our apartment—without a shirt. Just suspenders. He had a great chest.

NICKY

This is very kind—what you are all doing for Sergey.

VERA

It was George's idea.

NICKY

I know.

VERA

When he knew we'd be east.
To change the subject:

NATASHA

Let's set up the tables. It's warm enough out here, isn't it? They're working inside. But I think we should disturb them.

NICKY

I don't mind disturbing them. I'm an artist too!

Laughs. As he and NATASHA *head to the study:*

How many are we going to be?

NATASHA

I don't know. It just keeps growing.

> *They are gone, off the music suddenly stops.* VERA *sets her embroidery away, stands, she has been trying not to cry. She fixes her eyes.*
>
> LUCIA DAVIDOVA *(40s), also wearing an apron, enters from the house with tablecloths, candles etc. The music off has started again.*

LUCIA (*to* VERA)

Have you seen my niece?

VERA

I saw her in the study—.

LUCIA

Is she bothering them? I told her not to—.

VERA

I think she's turning pages for Igor. I don't think they mind. Let her watch, Lucia . . .

> NATASHA *and* NICKY *carry on a small desk from the house.*

LUCIA (*about the desk*)

I should have more tables . . .

NATASHA

This will work. This is fine . . .

LUCIA (*to* NATASHA)

My niece isn't bothering them?

VERA

They like the attention of young girls, Lucia. They're at that age.

NATASHA

What age isn't that?

Laughter.

When don't they . . .?

LUCIA (*to* NATASHA)

My niece should be helping . . .

> *Distant car.*

NATASHA (*looking off*)

Is that him? Is Kolya driving?

> *Suddenly they are excited and nervous, but before they
> can set up the tables:*

LUCIA (*looking off*)

It's just the girls. Where is he? I thought they were all coming
together. What happened?

> VLADIMIR SOKOLOFF (*50s*), LISA SOKOLOFF (*50s*), ALEKSI
> KARPOV *come out of the house, one or two still holding
> cards.*

VLADIMIR

Is he here?! We heard—.

LUCIA (*shaking her head*)

Natalia—.

NATASHA

And Evgenia.

LUCIA

Where is he?

NATASHA

We don't know.

VLADIMIR

Nicky—when did you get here?

> *Greetings.*

LUCIA

You know each other?

VLADIMIR

Who doesn't know Nicky? Everyone knows Nicky. Nicky knows
everyone.

> *As* NICKY *greets* LISA *and* VLADIMIR, *old friends he hasn't
> seen for years:*

NICKY

Not everyone.

NATASHA

Who doesn't Nicky know?

NICKY (*to* VLADIMIR)

I thought you were in a play.

NATASHA

He knew that.

> *Off the music has started again.*

LUCIA

He is.

VLADIMIR

I was in it. It closed!

LUCIA

It was very good.

VLADIMIR

No one wanted to see it.

LISA (*to* NICKY)

Are you here alone?

LUCIA (*to* NATASHA)

Nicky's still divorced.

NATASHA

I'm sorry for you, Nicky. (*to* LUCIA) I know.

NICKY

It's been two years. I'm over it.

LUCIA

Does anyone ever get over that?

LISA

Who was—[she]—?

NICKY

She was—.

NATASHA

I know. I know! Big breasted!

> *The women laugh at this.*

NICKY

Actually—she was, but that wasn't the only reason—I married . . .
her.

> *They aren't listening.*

> *The women are setting up the tables— to make one big
> table. Laying out the tablecloths, candles, etc.*

LISA

(*to the women*) Do you need me to help?

VLADIMIR

Help them.

He takes her cards from her.

Nicky, we are playing cards. Play my wife's hand.

Hands NICKY *the cards.*

NICKY

I hate cards.

Hands them back.

LUCIA *takes the napkins that* NICKY *has folded and refolds them.*

VLADIMIR (*to* KARPOV)

What are we going to do?

KARPOV

I don't. Maybe I know a game we can play . . .

As they head off into the house:

VLADIMIR

I tell people Nicky knows everything that is going on. You want to know—ask Nicky.

They are gone.

NICKY (*to* LISA)

Who does he tell? (*She ignores him. To* NATASHA, *about* KARPOV) I haven't seen Karpov for years. Does he still teach piano?

NATASHA *nods.*

He's gotten fat. And jowly. And a bit creepy.

NATASHA

We're engaged.

Before NICKY *can react,* EVGENIA (39) *and* NATALIA (35) *arrive with plates of baked goods, flowers, a bottle of wine.*

NATASHA

Evgenia, where is he?

EVGENIA

They're taking my car.

NATALIA (*about* EVGENIA's *car*)
In case it all proved too much for Sergey—

EVGENIA
—So Kolya can drive him back.

NATALIA
They left the same time we did . . . (*to* LUCIA) We got lost two times . . .

EVGENIA
We got lost!

NATALIA
It was my fault.

EVGENIA
Who gave us these directions?

LUCIA
There is nothing wrong with the directions . . .

VERA
How bad does Sergey look?

To change the subject:

LUCIA
(*introducing, changing the subject*) You know Nicky?

EVGENIA
We know Nicky.

NICKY (*making a joke*)
"Who doesn't know Nicky?"

NATASHA
I'm glad you agree.

Greetings.

(*introducing*) Mrs. Stravinsky.
VERA *and* EVGENIA *shake hands.*

LUCIA
Evgenia runs the ballet school.
Before she can protest:
That's what George says.

EVGENIA (*to* VERA, *pointing to* NATALIA)
She really does everything.

NATALIA (*shaking* VERA's *hand*)

I am the slave!

EVGENIA

We're eating out here? Nice. It's not too chilly?

NATASHA

Is it?

NATALIA

I'll put these in water.

> *She heads inside with the flowers.*

> *The women are setting the table.*

> *They go off and come back with plates, etc. It is all very efficient.*

LUCIA (*to* EVGENIA)

Do you think they'll be long?

EVGENIA

They were planning to leave at the same time.

> *Then:*

Maybe they had to stop.

LUCIA

What was wrong with the directions?

EVGENIA

Nothing was wrong . . . I wasn't driving . . .

> *Mimics her bad and slow driving.*

> *They work, then:*

(*to* VERA) George says you're here through the opening.

> VERA *nods. They work.*

I hadn't realized that Sergey had been your husband. George was telling me . . .

VERA

It was another life.

NATASHA

(*as she moves* NICKY *aside*) Nicky, you're in the way.

> *Pause.*

> NICKY *stands back and watches the women who go about this with great efficiency.*

NICKY

I can't help but say—what a lovely sight . . .

NATASHA

Oh God, don't say it, Nicky.

NICKY

What?

EVGENIA

What?

NATASHA (*to* NICKY)

Please don't talk about your childhood. (*to the others*) I heard this so many times. According to Nicky, his life has been one sad long downhill climb ever since he was a boy. When we were married—he said this to me all the time. I got sick of hearing it.

EVGENIA

You don't tell a wife that.

NICKY (*explaining*)

I had a very nice childhood.

NATASHA (*to the other women*)

With women always around—getting you things. Getting you everything. That's what he misses.

EVGENIA (*to* NICKY)

That's what you remember?

NICKY (*hesitates, then:*)

And it's a very good memory.

NATASHA (*to the women*)

See?

NICKY

What? What did I say? I thought it was a compliment. You reminded me of that . . .

As they continue to work:

NATASHA

He thinks he's funny. Help with the chairs, Nicky. (*to the others*) He never would help.

VERA

No wonder he can't keep a wife.

KARPOV *comes out of the house. He is now lugging a small table.*

KARPOV

Where do you want this?

LUCIA

Do we need another table?

KARPOV

George said to bring it out.

They add the table, and fix the tablecloths, etc.

Pause. Music off.

Vladimir doesn't want to play two-handed cards.

VLADIMIR *is in the doorway.*

(*referring to the music*) George is playing the piano for Igor now. (*then, to* VERA) They were just saying you hadn't seen Sergey in . . . A long time.

VERA

I won't be shocked. I've been warned. This is a very nice thing for George to do. For all of you to do.

Sound of a car driving up.

They stop, look off.

NATALIA *returns with the flowers in a vase.*

NATASHA (*to* KARPOV)

Get George.

KARPOV *goes inside.* LUCIA *runs off to the car.* VERA *tries to prepare herself.*

VERA (*to* NICKY)

I'm not going to get upset.

Pause, music plays off. All busy themselves as they wait.

KOLYA (SUDEIKIN'*s nephew, and* GEORGE'*s rehearsal pianist*) *enters, helping in* SERGEY SUDEIKIN, *who looks very unsteady, weak and unwell.*

LUCIA *tries to help too.*

LUCIA (*to* KOLYA)

Did you get lost?

KOLYA

We had to stop a few times.

A few muffled greetings, and kisses, then he sees VERA. *She smiles. She hugs him.*

The music continues off in starts and stops.

SUDEIKIN *starts to shake.*

VERA

Are you all right?

SUDEIKIN (*to* NATASHA)

She was my wife.

NATASHA

We know.

VLADIMIR *watches from the doorway.*

VERA (*to* SUDEIKIN)

We heard there was a party for you, and so we came.

SUDEIKIN

From California?

LUCIA

Just for this.

VERA

No. We were here.

SUDEIKIN

Your husband??

She points toward where the music is coming from.

VERA

Inside.

SUDEIKIN (*to* VERA)

You are looking very well.

VERA *doesn't respond.*

NATASHA (*responding for her*)

And so do you. And very handsome.

She looks to VERA *who is upset by how he looks, and can
hardly speak.*

EVGENIA (*over this*)

Sergey, sit. Please.

He sits, the others stand.
An awkward pause.

LUCIA

Who don't you know?

He looks around, smiles, a small wave, etc.

SUDEIKIN

I know everyone.

NATASHA

George and Igor have been working.

SUDEIKIN *just stares at* VERA. *She sits next to him.*

KOLYA

I'll tell them you're here.

He goes off to the study.

VERA

They know.

Awkward pause. No one knows what to do. Off the music stops. They look at each other, smile:

EVGENIA

Have you been here, to Lucia's house before?

LUCIA

No. He hasn't . . .

NATASHA

The table looks nice, doesn't it?

GEORGE BALANCHINE *(42)*, IGOR STRAVINSKY *(64), followed by* KARPOV *and* KOLYA *enter from the study.* IGOR *is putting on his jacket.* GEORGE *is tightening his cowboy "string" tie.*

And a few steps behind is ANNA, LUCIA's *19-year-old niece.*

GEORGE

Sergey Yurievich! How good it is to see you. Who said you were ill? Look at you! Look at you! How nice to see you . . .

GEORGE *hugs him, then:*

You don't have a drink—.

GEORGE *notices that* SUDEIKIN *is looking at* IGOR. *Everyone notices this, then:*

IGOR

Mr. Sudeikin.

SUDEIKIN, *with difficulty, starts to stand.*

GEORGE

Don't get up. Don't—.

SUDEIKIN *stands. Looks at* STRAVINSKY.

SUDEIKIN

Igor . . .

They shake hands.

(*to say something*) What are you working on?

NATASHA (*to* SERGEY)

Tea or something else?

VERA (*answering for him*)

Tea.

NATASHA *moves to go to the kitchen,* LUCIA *stops her.*

LUCIA

Anna, get the tea. And what were you doing in there?

ANNA

I was turning pages.

She goes inside.

GEORGE

You know everyone.

SUDEIKIN *looks around and then nods.*

(*to* NATASHA) How is our food? Lucia and Natasha have been watching our food.

NATASHA

George has been cooking for two days.

SUDEIKIN

Why?

NATASHA

For this. For you. (*then*) The food's ready. Should we get the food?

LUCIA

He just got here.

NATASHA (*to* SUDEIKIN)

You should sit back down.

LUCIA

Please, sit down.

VERA

Are you hungry, Sergey?

VERA *can't stop looking at* SUDEIKIN. *Others notice this.*

SUDEIKIN

Vera, do I look that bad?

GEORGE

It is not every day that we get so many old friends together. Everyone wanted to come.

NATASHA (*to* LUCIA)

Should we wait on the food?

LUCIA

I don't know. George?

GEORGE

Today there are more Russians in Westport than in Moscow.

Laughs, then:

Why don't we eat? Why wait? What are we waiting for? Sit down everyone. Let's sit down. Sergey's hungry after his long drive.

SUDEIKIN

I'm not hungry.

GEORGE

Well I am. We've been working, Sergey. Let's sit. Sit.

> ANNA *returns with the tea, she tries to hand it to* SUDEIKIN, *he ignores it;* VERA *takes it for him and sets it in front of him on the table, as:*
>
> *The men start to sit.* IGOR *tries to help* SUDEIKIN.

SUDEIKIN

I don't need your help.

VERA

Of course you don't . . .

SUDEIKIN (*to* GEORGE)

You did the cooking?

GEORGE

I did.

SUDEIKIN

Good.

LUCIA (*to* GEORGE)

Should we . . . ?

> GEORGE *nods.*

We'll bring the food.

> VERA *starts to stand.*

NATASHA (*to* VERA)

You stay there. We are fine.

> LUCIA, NATASHA, LISA, EVGENIA, NATALIA *and* ANNA *start to go in and out of the kitchen bringing plates and dishes and bowls of food.*

VLADIMIR (*about the food*)

Looks wonderful . . .

VERA (*to* SUDEIKIN)

Tomorrow we'll do something very special. For your name day. This—[the table] is only the beginning.

GEORGE

It's going to be a full weekend . . . Tomorrow is your name day . . .

Pause.

SUDEIKIN (*to* GEORGE)

Remember I used to stuff a pillow down my coat and imitate Diaghilev?

VERA

I remember that.

SUDEIKIN (*to* VERA, *about* GEORGE)

We met through Diaghilev. That's what made me think . . .

GEORGE

I don't think so, Sergey. When I worked for him you were already here in New York, weren't you? I could be wrong.

VERA (*to* SUDEIKIN, *explaining about* GEORGE)

Look how young he is. You couldn't have met him with Diaghilev.

NICKY

George used to imitate Diaghilev sometimes too. He'd pretend he had a monocle? Got all red in the face. Yelled at Lifar to take the buttons off his trousers!

Laughter by some, not by SUDEIKIN. ANNA *especially laughs.* LUCIA *sees this and sh-shs her.*

GEORGE (*explaining to* SERGEY)

Nicky and I met through Diaghilev.

SUDEIKIN

Lifar—was after my time.

Short pause.

EVGENIA

What did you do for Diaghilev, Sergey?

VERA (*answering for him*)

Salome. His sets were wonderful. You've kept the drawings, I hope.

SUDEIKIN (*shrugs*)

My apartment is a mess.

LUCIA

They could be worth something.

SUDEIKIN

They are worth something.

GEORGE

Your drawings are works of art . . . (*pointing out dishes to* SERGEY:)
Katletka. And pirozhki . . .

SUDEIKIN

I know the names.

NATASHA (*to the women*)

Maybe we should sit.

> *They are all seated, then.* NATASHA *suddenly realizes some-*
> *thing is missing and stands and hurries off to the kitchen.*

LUCIA (*calls after her*)

Anna can get it! (*to* ANNA) Niece. (*to the others*) She sat for maybe—
(*"looks" at her watch*) three seconds.

NICKY

She hasn't changed.

ANNA (*to* LUCIA)

Should I do something?

> *She is ignored.*
> *Food is being passed.* NATASHA *soon returns with another*
> *bowl and sits.*

LUCIA (*to say something, to* SUDEIKIN)

Sergey, George now gives some of the dancers money for steaks. He
says, to discourage them from putting on weight.

SUDEIKIN (*to* GEORGE)

You're doing all those musicals. So that's what pays.

VERA

George and Igor are talking about doing something new together.

NATASHA

More than just "talking." It's nearly done.

SUDEIKIN

A musical?

GEORGE

No, no.

VERA

Igor doing a musical?

IGOR

I could do a musical.

Laughter.

GEORGE

A new ballet.

SUDEIKIN (*eating*)

What's the story?

IGOR

Why couldn't I do a musical?

GEORGE

Orpheus.

They eat.

SUDEIKIN (*smiles, to* GEORGE)

You never give up.

IGOR (*a look at* GEORGE, *then:*)

Why do you say that? What does he mean?

GEORGE

I did an *Orpheus* for the Met about ten years ago. You have a very
good memory, Sergey.

SUDEIKIN

I can always remember my friends' failures.

IGOR (*to* NICKY)

Gluck?

NICKY *nods.*

NATASHA

It was wonderful. George put the opera singers in the pit and only
the dancers on the stage.

IGOR

I'm sure the Met loved that.

Short pause.

SUDEIKIN (*to* IGOR)

I finally saw your cartoon, Igor.

IGOR

I didn't have anything to do with—.

SUDEIKIN

Dinosaurs. Not what I picture when I hear *Rite of Spring*. But I suppose now I will.

Eats, then:

I suppose now the world will. (*to the table, explaining*) Everyone needs money.

Then:

Yes, do a musical . . .

SUDEIKIN *is not eating,* LUCIA *tries to point out other dishes:*

LUCIA

Schuba. Salade Olivier.

SUDEIKIN (*to* GEORGE)

I want Kirstein to give me a job. I've worked for him. Why doesn't he hire me again?

No response.

Maybe for this ballet you and Igor are doing.

Short pause.

GEORGE

We're almost done, Sergey. We open in a couple of weeks. We have a designer.

Short pause.

IGOR (*eating*)

Orpheus has a mask—makes him look like a catcher on a baseball team. I had to throw a fit.

EVGENIA

The set is a lot of big rocks. Beautiful big rocks.

GEORGE

And a curtain. A silk billowing curtain. Kirstein didn't want to pay for the curtain. Nicky found the money for us.

SUDEIKIN *looks at* NICKY.

NICKY

It wasn't much.

IGOR

You need help, Nicky is there to help. God bless, Nicky.

SUDEIKIN (*to* NICKY)

Can you help me?

NICKY *doesn't know what to say.*

LUCIA (*changing the subject*)

I thought of inviting Lincoln today.

NATASHA

He doesn't speak Russian.

GEORGE

That's why I didn't.

VLADIMIR

It's so nice to be only speaking Russian.

NATALIA

It's nice just to have us.

SUDEIKIN (*to* NICKY)

Where did you find the money for George's curtain?

NICKY *looks to* GEORGE.

GEORGE

Show him your card. Nika has a job now, Sergey. He even has a card.

NICKY *hands* SUDEIKIN *his card.*

SUDEIKIN (*handing it to* KOLYA)

What does it say? I don't have my glasses.

KOLYA

"Voice of America—for Russia."

SUDEIKIN

I didn't know countries had voices. (*to* IGOR) What do you think ours is? Baritone? Bass?

Laughs.

KOLYA

What do you mean by "ours?"

Laughter.

IGOR

Careful. We must all be Americans here.

He looks to NICKY, *smiles.*

NICKY (*smiling*)

I'm not a spy! I have a job in the government.

NATASHA

When did this happen? I didn't know about this, Nicky.
(*to* LUCIA) Did you?

LUCIA

I heard something about—.

NICKY

Heard what?

KARPOV (*to* NICKY)

What do you do?

IGOR

He helps people. He helps Russians. (*a joke*) His web reaches far
and wide.

NICKY

I don't have a "web."

LISA

Can we see that? [the card]

NATASHA (*to* IGOR)

"He helps Russians?" What does that mean?

As the card is passed around:

GEORGE

He bought us a curtain! (*to* SERGEY) I had no idea how I was going
to get the dead Eurydice off the stage—without that curtain.

LUCIA

A beautiful silk billowy curtain.

SUDEIKIN

Why couldn't she just crawl behind one of your designer's big ugly
rocks?

He laughs.

EVGENIA

The rocks aren't—[ugly].

SUDEIKIN's *laugh suddenly turns into a cough. Others
try to ignore this. It's a mean cough. He settles down. He
looks around the table.*

SUDEIKIN (*wiping his mouth*)

So many—Russians.

LUCIA

That's what George was saying. It's nice.

KARPOV

Nicky, can I keep this? [the card]

GEORGE (*to* SERGEY)

Later, if you'd like, Igor and I can show you some of what we've done. We're planning on it.

LISA

Nicky, do you have any more cards?

NICKY *passes out cards as:*

SUDEIKIN *is smiling to himself, about to say something to the table.*

VERA

What, Sergey? You want to say something?

SUDEIKIN *looks to* EVGENIA.

SUDEIKIN

You. What can you remember?

EVGENIA *and the others are confused.*

GEORGE

Do you mean about—home?

SUDEIKIN *nods.*

LISA (*to* GEORGE)

How did you know he meant—?

GEORGE (*to the table*)

He means about home.

SUDEIKIN (*to* EVGENIA)

What? What do you remember?

GEORGE

Evgenia was a princess. Would have been a princess.

EVGENIA

I was a child.

LUCIA

Natasha was a princess.

NATASHA

I think I still am.

Laughter.

Don't laugh so hard, Nicky.

NICKY (*to* KARPOV)
Did you know you were marrying a Princess?

SUDEIKIN
Anyone else?

NATASHA
Nicky grew up in the biggest house.

NICKY
I think I did.

LUCIA
And we know he had a lot of women serving him.
    Laughter.

NATASHA
He lost his virginity with the maid.
    She smiles.

GEORGE (*under his breath, as a joke*)
Droit de seigneur!

NICKY (*to* NATASHA)
That was told in some confidence . . .
    Smiles.
When you were my wife . . .

SUDEIKIN (*to* ANNA)
What about you? You're very pretty. What's your name?

ANNA
Anna.

LUCIA
She's my niece.

SUDEIKIN
Were you born here?
    She shakes her head.

LUCIA
France.

SUDEIKIN
You can't answer for yourself?

ANNA
France.

SUDEIKIN (*not a question*)

So you've never been—home.

Turns back to the others:

When I came here . . .

GEORGE

I think you were the first, weren't you?

VERA

I think he was.

GEORGE (*looking to* VLADIMIR)

Vladimir . . .

VLADIMIR

He was before me.

SUDEIKIN

I left and—Verochka sent me a postcard.

She shakes her head, she doesn't remember this.

She doesn't remember. It said, "You are approaching New York and can see the Statue of Liberty. May she bring you victory."

Others look at him, he tries not to be upset.

Victory . . .

GEORGE

And it did.

SUDEIKIN (*to* VERA)

And you'd left me for Igor, because you said I wasn't famous enough.

He smiles.

She looks at him:

VERA

I don't think I said that.

GEORGE (*change of subject*)

Once with Diaghilev—we were talking about him—I was in the wings with Spessiva.

To NATASHA *and* LUCIA:

I've told this—.

LUCIA

Tell it.

NICKY (*over this*)

I remember Spessiva.

GEORGE

A *Swan Lake* I think. I tell her, "Dancers must never fall. Once you fall on stage you can never build up again. You have to fight too hard to make an audience forget a fall." She nods. She agrees. Then she runs on stage and immediately falls over.

Laughter, especially ANNA *who draws another dirty look from her aunt.*

SUDEIKIN (*seeming out of the blue*)

Igor—I have been told that you take pictures of Verochka naked.

Awkward pause.

IGOR

I used to. And she of me—naked.

SUDEIKIN

I'd like to see them. The ones of her, not of you.

IGOR

When you are next in California.

He eats.

I keep them in an album.

SUDEIKIN (*to* GEORGE)

Diaghilev touched a painting with his eyes, like a cook at a market touching a carrot—will it be good enough for the soup?

The table eats, SUDEIKIN *remembers:*

Verochka sold her pear diamond earrings for 3,000 Kerensky rubles —that's how we got to Marseille. We arrived in Paris during the celebration of Jeanne d'Arc becoming a saint. It felt like we'd landed on the moon.

VERA *nods and takes his hand.*

VERA

That is what it felt like.

GEORGE (*gestures for him to come to him*)

Kolya . . .

KOLYA *stands and goes to* GEORGE *as:*

SUDEIKIN (*another memory*)

Verochka in the Crimea. We were waiting . . .

To IGOR

Has she told you any of this?

NICKY

That's where my family waited. The Crimea. Then we went to Nice.

EVGENIA

We had a villa in Nice. It was like we were on a holiday. That just went on and on. Waiting to go home . . .

> GEORGE *whispers something to* KOLYA, *who heads off into the house.*

NATASHA (*to* GEORGE)

What . . . ?

> GEORGE *sh-shs her, to listen to* SERGEY:

SUDEIKIN (*continuing*)

She painted silhouettes on glass. She said she wanted an art that was fragile.

VERA (*smiling*)

I did.

SUDEIKIN (*another story*)

When the great Karsavina played in my *Salome*, I painted a rose myself on her knee before every performance.

> *From inside, a record begins to play: S. Taneyev's choral piece,* Dawn. *[written at the turn of the century, it is a moving and deeply spiritual piece for male and female chorus.]*

SUDEIKIN

The boat we sailed off in—to leave, Vera. Tiny, full of oil drums. Then a storm. We landed not in Constantinople, in Batrum, the other side of the Black Sea. And traveled through Baku. Where the women wore veils . . .

NICKY (*quietly*)

I know this . . .

> *The music stops* SUDEIKIN *for a moment;* KOLYA *returns.*

GEORGE

Is it too loud? I thought it would be nice to have in the background.

> *They listen.*

Igor, do you know this?

IGOR

Taneyev. Where did you find it?

GEORGE

Lucia—.

LUCIA

I found it at one of the bookshops on Third Avenue.

They listen.

EVGENIA

Which one?

LUCIA

Pageant?

They listen.

GEORGE

We can still talk—.

NICKY

I—sang this.

NATASHA

What??

NICKY

In school. I was in the chorus. We wore little blue jackets. It's called *Dawn*. I couldn't have been more than ten. (*to* IGOR) You didn't know Taneyev, did you?

IGOR

I met him. Once. He was an old man then.

NATALIA

When did he die?

IGOR

Just before the—the hell.

VERA

Lucky man.

They listen.

IGOR

He came to the school. Rimsky knew him. So he came.

Suddenly SUDEIKIN *gets up, others try to help him, he won't be helped.*

He goes off inside. The others are confused. They assume he is going to turn it off.

GEORGE

I didn't mean . . . I thought he'd like it . . .

LUCIA

Kolya.

> KOLYA *hurries inside. But then suddenly the music is much louder and* SUDEIKIN *comes out. He has turned it way up.* KOLYA *follows him out.*

SUDEIKIN

We are in the woods. Who's going to complain . . . ?

> *As the music reaches its thrilling and moving conclusion, all are still, listening, deeply moved by all they know they have lost. Tears pour down* SERGEY's *face.* NATALIA *points this out to* EVGENIA *who then gets a handkerchief from her purse and tries to give it to* SERGEY, *who won't take it.*
>
> *They listen until the music ends.*

GEORGE

Sergey, when's the last time you've been to church?

SUDEIKIN (*to* VERA)

George is trying to get me to go to church.

> *He is pouring himself some vodka.*

VERA

You shouldn't be drinking vodka.

NATASHA

Isn't it too late for that?

SUDEIKIN

Why is it late?

LUCIA

Too late for what?

NATASHA

Church.

NICKY

How long is the service? I forget.

GEORGE

Nikolai Dimitrievich, you should go too. Before you forget everything.

NICKY

Too late for that. Have they put seats in yet?

Laughter.

GEORGE

No.

KOLYA

When you go, go with George. In that church everyone knows him.
I went with him once, he walks in and it's the Tsar.

ANNA

I go to church.

She eats.

SUDEIKIN (*smiling, to* GEORGE)

So how was France?

GEORGE

We got back ages ago. All that's been forgotten.

SUDEIKIN (*to the others*)

It was that bad.

Smiles.

LUCIA

He wasn't going to live there. It was just for the six months.

SUDEIKIN

That's not what I heard.

LUCIA (*to* NICKY)

George wants to live here. Not France.

NICKY

Why are you saying that to me?

Short pause.

SUDEIKIN

I'm sorry to hear you don't like your designer. Who is it?

IGOR

He's Japanese. He was Kirstein's idea.

SUDEIKIN (*getting feisty, to* GEORGE)

And where's your young wife?

GEORGE

She's coming. Later. She doesn't speak Russian. You'll see her dance.

EVGENIA

Maria is Eurydice.

SUDEIKIN

So she gets all the good parts now.
>   *Smiles.*

And what do you call yourself now?

GEORGE

What do you mean?

SUDEIKIN

Every time I bump into Kirstein, you've got a different name.

IGOR

What are you now "Society of Ballet?

EVGENIA & NATALIA (*correcting him*)

Ballet Society.

VERA

Igor, please. They work for Kirstein.

SUDEIKIN (*laughing*)

He just keeps changing the names! Like re-arranging the chairs on a boat that's about to sink . . .
>   *Smiles, then:*

The money has always just run through Lincoln's fingers. At least when his father could keep him on an allowance . . . Now I hear his mother just . . . Mothers . . .

NATALIA

That's not true. And careful what you say—.

EVGENIA

Why does he have to be careful?

SUDEIKIN

He can't even buy you a curtain, George.

IGOR (*to* SUDEIKIN)

And now he's not even selling tickets, Sergey.

EVGENIA

And that's not true.

IGOR

You have to become some—member or something.

EVGENIA

That's right.

IGOR

And Sergey—he's got them performing on only the best nights. On Monday *and* Tuesday nights!! The "best" nights of the week!

SUDEIKIN *laughs.*

EVGENIA

Because it's cheaper.

IGOR

I guessed that.

GEORGE

At least we're out of the Auditorium of the High School for Needle Trades!!

Laughter.

SUDEIKIN (*to* VERA)

Is that what that place was called?

GEORGE (*a joke*)

Lincoln himself swept that stage of needles!

EVGENIA

No, he didn't.

NATALIA

We did!

Laughter.

IGOR

We're now in the City Center, Sergey. Have you worked there?

SUDEIKIN *shakes his head.*

The pit smells like a men's toilet.

Short pause.

Then:

GEORGE

I did miss things when we were in Paris.

This gets their attention.

LUCIA

What things, George?

GEORGE

I missed the way they move here, Sergey. The girls.

LUCIA

Oh god. (*explaining*) The girls.

VERA

What?

GEORGE

The girls here. How they walk. So—unselfconscious here. You don't
find that in France.

IGOR

No.

VLADIMIR

No.

GEORGE

Like they've practiced every move.

NATASHA

How did this start?

LUCIA (*getting up*)

They're going to start talking about girls.

ANNA

What?

LUCIA

They always do.

LISA

But we're right here?

LUCIA

Oh they don't care. Or notice. (*to the women*) Help me with these.
We'll get the next course . . .

GEORGE (*ignoring them*)

Long-legged athletic American girls . . .

LUCIA

Are we done with this?

She starts to pick up some dishes.

IGOR (*to the men*)

George was telling me earlier—.

LUCIA (*to the women*)

Let's take these into the kitchen. Come with us, Anna. It's where we belong . . .

> *The women are standing, picking up things, the men pretend to be oblivious.*

IGOR (*continuing*)

When he was in Paris. Not this time. A long time ago. And the Negro performer—Josephine . . .

NICKY

I know who you mean.

KOLYA

Baker.

NICKY

Baker.

VLADIMIR (*to* NICKY)

Do you know her?

NICKY

No, I—.

KARPOV

Someone Nicky doesn't know!

IGOR

She invites George to her apartment, for dinner. And she cooks him spaghetti—without a stitch of clothes on.

NATASHA

My god . . .

> NATASHA *is the last to leave and now the women are gone.*

SUDEIKIN (*to* GEORGE)

Is that true?

> GEORGE *nods, then the punchline:*

GEORGE

Sergey, she was very domestic.

> *They laugh.* ANNA *and* LISA *have come out to pick up a few things.* GEORGE *hands* ANNA *a dish. Then to the men:*

Igor, was telling me—Tell them.

IGOR

What?

GEORGE

About your first child. He was telling me while we were working this morning. What made you think of—?

IGOR

I don't know. I think of it all the time.

> LISA *is about to go into the house,* ANNA *is listening in the doorway.*

LISA

Come and help, Anna.
> ANNA *goes inside.*

GEORGE

He's taken to—it's some kind of employment agency.

IGOR (*taking over the story*)

In a grungy basement office.

GEORGE

This is because his wife doesn't have enough milk.

VLADIMIR

My wife was like that.

IGOR

And they are lined up.

KARPOV (*confused, to* VLADIMIR)

Who?

VLADIMIR (*explaining to* KARPOV)

Wet nurses.

KARPOV

Wet nurses . . .

GEORGE

He's maybe—twenty-four?

IGOR

And—I was so so innocent. A real babe in the woods.
> *They laugh.*

KARPOV

I was that way too.

IGOR

I knew nothing about . . .

KARPOV

Me too! Nothing.

NICKY

Our maid taught me—.

VLADIMIR

We heard, Nicky.

IGOR

So imagine: the girls are lined up. A very fat official woman, she
stands with me . . .

KOLYA

These sorts of women always scared me.

IGOR *sort of acts all of this out:*

IGOR

We look down the line of these eight, nine girls, women. She says to
them—"Now." Each one [demonstrates]. And now they are all naked
from the waist.

VLADIMIR

You must have thought you'd gone to heaven, Igor.

NATASHA *in the doorway.*

NATASHA (*to* GEORGE)

Should we bring out the next course, George? It's ready.

He gestures to bring it out. She goes off again.

IGOR

Naked. The whole line of them.

NICKY (*to* VLADIMIR)

And an innocent babe—.

GEORGE

It's a true story.

KARPOV (*to* NICKY)

I never saw a naked breast until I was . . .

IGOR

And we, this fat woman and me—and I'm shaking now, I'm that
nervous—

VLADIMIR

I'll bet you were.

KARPOV

I would be! (*reaches for a dish, to* NICKY) Hand me the pirozhki . . .

NICKY

They're bringing the next—.

IGOR

She leads me along; we walk this line like we're inspecting soldiers.

The women start to come out: first NATASHA *and* ANNA *with large dishes covered by cloth.*

When we've seen them all, she hands me—a cup.

KARPOV

I knew he was going to say that.

IGOR

I start to hand it to the first girl, but the fat official woman says: "No."

Then NATALIA *and* EVGENIA *enter with large dishes covered with cloth.*

IGOR

I'm supposed to hold it. The cup. Under.

LUCIA *and* VERA *come out with dishes.*

So one by one, each girl she [demonstrates: squeezes her breast] . . . and then I . . . drink it. Make some self-conscious stupid gesture of— "nice" or "good." "I like the vintage."

Laughter.

KARPOV

You didn't say that.

IGOR *picks up a glass.*

IGOR

Cup about the size of this glass.

NICKY

I had at least three wet nurses. They said I was always hungry.

As the women set out the food:

NATASHA (*pointing out the dishes*)

Lamb gorochayve. Srasi . . . Strogonoff . . .

KARPOV

I miss Russia . . .

Lights fade.

Scene Two

The same, the porch. Early evening.

The tables are either pushed back or gone.

Off, from the study—music; KOLYA *is playing a section of the score for* IGOR, GEORGE *and other guests.*

VERA *embroiders;* NICKY *sits with* LUCIA *and* LISA SOKOLOFF

SUDEIKIN *is now asleep in a chair.*

They listen to the music.

Pause.

The music finishes.

LISA (*to* NICKY)
What do you do again? I don't think I understand.

NICKY
I'm mostly a composer.

LISA
I know that. But—.
Turns to VERA
Vera, what does he do?

VERA (*embroidering*)
He helps us with our problems, Lisa.
She smiles at NICKY
(*to* LISA) You saw his card?

LISA
I saw it.
Off, a new section of music has started.

NICKY (*to* LISA)
And I compose.
They listen for a moment, then:

VERA
(*explaining the music they are hearing*) This is when Orpheus is leading his wife out of Hades. The Dark Angel has Orpheus' lyre—that guides them. Orpheus and Eurydice are dancing this.

LUCIA

I love this. George is doing wonderful things with this.

VERA

I am sure.

Continuing to LISA:

Orpheus of course can't see, he has the mask on—.

NICKY

The catcher's mask.

He smiles, VERA *doesn't.*

Just the thought of Igor telling his Japanese designer that his mask
looks—.

VERA

They're changing that. He has on some mask—so it's all touch.

LISA

Very nice.

NATASHA *and* ANNA *come out of the house, with a tray of
coffee and cake.*

VERA

We just ate.

NATASHA (*to* LUCIA)

It's like home in there. All your icons.

LUCIA (*nods and, puts her finger to her lips*)

Sh-sh . . .

They listen to the music for a moment, then:

VERA (*continuing about the music*)

Eurydice is frustrated. Because Orpheus can't see her. That makes
her feel—or them—distant from each other. It'll brighten as
Eurydice dances in front of a blind Orpheus.

NICKY (*moved*)

What an idea. My god . . .

They listen.

SUDEIKIN *snores.*

VERA (*touches him*)

You are snoring.

SUDEIKIN

No, I'm not.

He closes his eyes.

VERA

He's resting up for the big day tomorrow.

LISA *(continues)*

So all this was worked out—before George even began—?

NATASHA

They went back and forth—meeting in the city, George went to Los
Angeles—. Over a year now . . .

LUCIA

Almost two. They're still working out some things—as you'll see.

They listen for a moment:

VERA *(continuing)*

Orpheus is caught up in the dance. Eurydice is right in front of him,
but he can't look. He feels her against him, touching him, wanting
him. He longs to see her, but if he looks, she'll die. George told
Igor—she's like a memory.

MARIA TALLCHIEF *(23)*, GEORGE's *wife, is in the doorway
to the house. She stops. She is at first unnoticed.*

[NOTE: *Maria speaks no Russian. When others talk to her
in English, they speak with accents—this is in <u>under-
scored italics</u>.*]

She touches his face. Orpheus tries to hold her. They only get more
frustrated. Orpheus suddenly can't bear it, and tears the mask off
his face.

Music finishes.

She falls. And she dies.

Short pause.

MARIA

That's my pas de deux.

The others turn to her, surprised.

LUCIA

<u>Maria! We did not hear your car!</u>

To NATASHA:

Did you hear a car?

NATASHA

No.

They are getting up and greeting.

LUCIA

You look so beautiful.

MARIA

Lucia, what a lovely home—.

VERA

Maria—.

MARIA

Madam Stravinsky . . .

They greet.

LUCIA (*at the same time*)

Your husband's inside.

MARIA

I can hear . . . Nicholas has already run off into the woods. He took one step out of the car and cried: "Nature!"

She laughs.

LUCIA (*gesturing toward* SUDEIKIN:)

Shhh . . .

MARIA (*quietly*)

We spend too much time in the city. This is a real treat.

LISA

Who's Nicholas?

ANNA

The Orpheus.

LUCIA

Sit, Maria. Sit. Anna will show you where you're staying in a minute. Anna is my niece . . .

MARIA (*to* ANNA)

A pleasure to meet you.

LUCIA

And Nicky—.

NICKY

We've met many times . . .

LUCIA

The directions were fine?

MARIA

We had no problem at all.

LUCIA (*to* NATASHA)

Why did Evgenia have such a problem?

LISA (*to* NATASHA, *in Russian*)

This is George's wife?

NATASHA

The newest one.

LISA

And she speaks no Russian?

NATASHA

Not a word.

She shakes her head.

LISA *looks at* MARIA *and smiles,* MARIA *smiles back.*

ANNA

That's a beautiful dress, Miss Tallchief.

MARIA

Thank you.

LUCIA (*to* NATASHA)

She could wear a sack.

LISA

She's the Indian?

They look at her.

MARIA

What?

LUCIA

She's the Indian.

NATASHA *smiles.*

LISA (*to* NATASHA)

What Natasha?

NATASHA

George and I were on a train, going across the country and we
passed through an Indian reservation and George shouted out

the window: "Look—my relatives!"
The Russian women laugh.

MARIA

What? I don't understand.

NATASHA

Nothing, Maria.

VERA (*to* MARIA)
They are saying we've been so looking forward to seeing you.

NATASHA (*to* LISA)
Another time, he just blurts out—out of nowhere: "I feel like I have married America!"
They laugh.

LUCIA (*laughing*)
Oh George!

LISA
Is that why he's wearing those funny ties now?

VERA (*to* LISA)
You haven't met?
LISA *shakes her head.*
Forgive me, Maria. This is Lisa. She's my best friend in America.

MARIA
How do you do?

VERA
And so now you get all the good roles.

MARIA
I hope so.
She smiles.
I say to George—make me look beautiful. This is all I ask.
She laughs to herself.

VERA
I think you are very beautiful.

MARIA
I have a large head. It's out of proportion, with my body. Somehow, George—when I dance—he makes it look smaller.

VERA

Does he. Is that what he tells you?

MARIA *nods.*

I'd like to see how he does that.

LUCIA

(*to* LISA *and* VERA, *shaking her head*) Dancers.

LISA

How old is she?

MARIA

What?? (*to* VERA) What did she say?

VERA (*to* MARIA, in English)

She was saying how attractive you are, Maria.

LISA (*to* ANNA)

Is she your age?

ANNA

Oh, she's older. Maybe twenty-one?

NATASHA

Have a piece of cake.

MARIA (*categorical*)

Oh I don't eat cake.

   Women look at each other.

LISA (*in Russian*)

Give her a big piece.

VERA (*to* MARIA)

Lisa's husband is an actor.

MARIA (*smiling to* LISA)

I know a lot of actors. Maybe I know your husband.

LISA

What do you think would happen if one of us, Vera, divorced our
husband and married a skinny teenage boy?

NICKY

You think she's that young?

LUCIA

Ask her. She will tell you anything.

   NATASHA *smiles.*

LISA

What? What do you mean?

LUCIA

Once we were leaving a restaurant, and she turns to George—right in front of us—she asks him if he had to go to the bathroom.

MARIA

What are you talking about?

NICKY

Nothing. Nothing.

LUCIA (*over* NICKY)

And she tells us—and George—is still there—that George never admits having to go to the bathroom. It embarrasses him.

NATASHA

She seems to say whatever comes into her head.

MARIA (*standing, to* ANNA)

I should freshen up, after the trip. Maybe even lie down for a bit.

NATASHA

Yes, you are dancing tonight. You must rest.

LUCIA

Anna will show you to your room. Anna, show her George's room.

MARIA *and* ANNA *start to leave.*

ANNA

We are so happy you are here, Miss Tallchief.

MARIA (*to* ANNA)

All this, it just feels so—(looks back at the women) Russian . . .

MARIA *and* ANNA *go inside.*

LUCIA

What does she mean by that?

LISA

I don't know.

NATASHA

We never get to spend time with her in the city. Is George hiding her from us?

LUCIA

Why would he do that?

LISA

She didn't even touch her cake . . .

Short pause.

LUCIA (*to* NATASHA)

Tell Lisa about your talk with . . .

Smiles at MARIA *who smiles back.*

NATASHA

He asked me to talk with her.

LUCIA

Listen to this.

She laughs.

LISA

What?

NATASHA

Before he asked her to marry him. George is confused because Maria won't sleep with George. He is "hinting" pretty damn hard—but she won't. He's not sure if she is turning him down, or if she just doesn't understand. I talk to her. And I come back to George and give him the bad news—she's not going to sleep with anyone, except a husband.

Laughter.

LUCIA

We think he was attracted by the novelty.

Laughter.
The music starts again.
They listen for a moment.

LUCIA

They've jumped to the end.

They listen.

LISA

What happens at the end?

LUCIA

Apollo's at his son's grave. This is not part of the myth. George thought of this. And Orpheus' lyre is there. And then it just starts to rise up and up.

LISA

His lyre?

They listen.

What are they trying to say—that music is too good for this world?

NATASHA

They don't talk like that.

NICKY

Or maybe—art rises above . . .

Off the music ends.

Short pause.

LUCIA (*standing*)

We should get Evgenia and Natalia to help . . . Someone will be wanting to play cards. And all the tables are out here . . .

NATASHA

I'll find them . . .

She starts to go inside.

LUCIA

In the kitchen . . .

GEORGE *is in the doorway, with* NICHOLAS MAGALLANES (*26*), *a handsome young man and dancer. He, like* MARIA, *speaks no Russian.*

NATASHA *stops and listens.*

GEORGE (*to the women*)

Look who's here.

The women shake NICHOLAS's *hand*

GEORGE *goes to* SUDEIKIN *and gently wakes him:*

Sergey? Sergey? (*no response*) Sergey? Look who's here?

SUDEIKIN *wakes:*

SUDEIKIN

What? (*waking up, angry*) What?!

GEORGE

Look who is here to see you, Sergey.

GEORGE *gestures to* NICHOLAS *to come onto the porch.*

SUDEIKIN *lights up.*

He just appeared in the doorway while we were working . . .

SUDEIKIN

Like an angel.

NICHOLAS

What?

GEORGE

He says you are like an angel.
(*to* SUDEIKIN) He's going to dance for you later. This is your treat.

KARPOV, VLADIMIR *and* KOLYA *have come out of the house
to watch.*

SUDEIKIN (*staring at* NICHOLAS)

Thank you. Thank you.

VLADIMIR

We think you've slept enough, Sergey. The day is still young.

NATALIA *and* EVGENIA *enter with* NATASHA.

GEORGE

And we're about to open refreshments in the study.

VERA

He shouldn't drink.

GEORGE

Why?

NATALIA (*to* LUCIA)

They're moving inside?

LUCIA *nods.*

NATALIA *and* EVGENIA *begin to move a table back inside.*

GEORGE (*to* SUDEIKIN, *getting him up*)

We're done working. We are going to have "refreshments." We are
going to play cards. We'll tell stories. We want to hear yours.

SUDEIKIN (*standing up*)

I have a lot of stories.

GEORGE

We know. We know . . .

NATALIA *and* EVGENIA *carry the table inside.*

GEORGE *has to help* SUDEIKIN.

GEORGE

You're not too tired?

SUDEIKIN

No, no.

GEORGE

Then let's go inside . . .

SUDEIKIN *moves slowly.*

Did you like Igor's music?

SUDEIKIN *is confused.*

VERA

You've been asleep.

SUDEIKIN

No, I haven't.

As they wait:

GEORGE (*to the women*)

Where's my wife? I saw her out here . . .

LUCIA

She's changing.

GEORGE (*to the women*)

I hope you behaved yourselves.

Then to fill the time it takes for SUDEIKIN *to cross to the door:*

KOLYA

I'll start with a story. George and I took a trip to Cuba together. And he refused to buy a Spanish phrase book. Because—

GEORGE (*helping* SUDEIKIN *across the room to the door*)

Kolya . . .

KOLYA

Because, according to George, all you had to do is add "ados" to any English word and the Cubans would understand. You want a match—you say "matchados."

Everyone is watching the slow and painful walk across the room by SUDEIKIN.

A glass of milk—"milkados." He called this Balanchine Spanish.

SUDEIKIN

That's very funny . . .

And they go inside. KOLYA *quickly follows.*
KARPOV, VLADIMIR, NICKY *and the others remain.*

VLADIMIR

Did he hear any of Igor's music?

LISA

I don't know what he heard . . .

As NATASHA, LUCIA *and* LISA *have picked up what remains*
—the last table, and a few things.
NATASHA *stops:*

NATASHA

I visited him in his apartment for the first time—just a week or so
ago. It's a real shit hole. On East 73rd. He'd worked for Diaghilev.
He showed me a couple of paintings. The only ones left, he said.
Pulled them out of a closet. One was completely ruined. The other
maybe can be fixed.

To NICKY, VLADIMIR, KARPOV.

Bring in the chairs . . .

LUCIA

I'd like to hear his stories.

Carrying the table inside:

NATASHA

Before they're forgotten. Before they're gone . . .

They are all heading inside, except for VERA *and* KARPOV.
VLADIMIR *and* NICKY *with chairs.*

VERA (*she embroiders*)

Nicky? Before you go can I talk to you for a minute.

NICKY *stops.*

KARPOV

I was going to ask the same thing, Nicky. I'll wait inside.

Then, picking up chairs.

I'll bring in these chairs . . .

He takes a couple of chairs inside.

NICKY *sets down his chairs.*

VERA *and* NICKY *are alone.*

A crowd now in the study listening—from there—
a burst of laughter.

NICKY

A wonderful meal . . . I think we've made Sergey very happy.

VERA (*she nods, then:*)

You're going to miss all the stories . . . And the cards . . .

NICKY

I hate cards.

Then. They are alone.

Do you need help? Does Igor?

Then:

VERA

Coming home from Mexico—where Igor had a concert—they took me to another room, at the border. Igor was furious.

Then:

They said I'd lied on my application for citizenship. That I'd never been divorced—officially—from Sergey. And so wasn't legally married—to Igor.

Short pause.

NICKY

Is that true?

VERA

We couldn't get the papers, Nicky . . . Sergey and I had been married in Russia. There wasn't a Russia anymore . . .

NICKY

I understand.

VERA

They said—the one time. They'd let me in. But the next time . . . What am I going to do, Nika? I can't ever leave?

Then:

I didn't tell Igor about this. I just said there had been a confusion because of the Russian names. How to spell them.

She embroiders.

Is this the sort of thing you do?

NICKY

It is.

She looks at him.

VERA

Thank you.

Burst of laughter from the other room.

Thank you.

NICKY

I'll let you know when it's sorted out.

VERA *sighs, and sets down her embroidery.*

Vera—isn't it lovely here?

She nods.

I remember on name days, when I was a boy—we'd hire a Jewish band from the village. Violin, zither, maybe guitar, accordion. We'd sit outside. On the porch.

Gestures: like this.

And listen to them play from the house. And we'd do plays. Around this time. Around Easter. My family. I remember one year they did *The Bear*. I was maybe ten.

Turns to VERA.

Your husband is an important person—they know that here. I'll write a few letters . . . Don't worry.

Then, she hasn't moved.

Something else?

VERA

They have letters Igor wrote—before the war. When we were going to move to Italy. He wrote letters. He said a lot of things. He even sent that man a birthday present.

NICKY *thinks, then:*

NICKY

Did he ever—visit Mussolini?

VERA

Yes.

Then:

He got a call from immigration. What do they want him to do? They don't say.

Then:

He took his name off of a concert. He's no longer sponsoring that.

NICKY

For Hans Eisler. Hans Eisler is a communist. I heard about that. We have to be careful.

VERA

He's no longer a sponsor of that concert, Nicky. So is that the kind of thing they want him to do? He doesn't know.

NICKY

That was a good thing to do. Yes. Things like that. Be—helpful. They notice. So they help. Makes it easier for me to help.

VERA

Upstairs, in our room—.

NICKY

What? What else?

VERA

I told Igor this wasn't going to—. Do anything. But, you know my husband. He thinks—.

NICKY

What's upstairs, Vera?

VERA

I have some music he wants me to give you.

NICKY

To give me?

VERA

Igor's done—. He got it into his head . . . It's a new arrangement— for the "Star Spangled Banner." He wants to offer it to the President. Maybe, he thinks, it could become a new official version? What do you think?

Short pause.

NICKY

I don't know Mr. Truman—personally. But I'd be honored to take the music . . . I'll do everything I can. I'm sure it's—very special. Better than what we've got.

She relaxes, stands and goes and kisses NICKY *on the cheek.*

VERA

Igor says you are his very good friend, Nika. Our friend. Your couch is always ready for you in Hollywood. He lets no one else sleep on it. Thank you.

She smiles.

NICKY

Vera, I can't tell you how much I cherish the time I spend with Igor and you. Please, don't worry.

She goes in.

Immediately KARPOV *peeks his head in.*

KARPOV

Is this a good time?

NICKY *turns to him.*

NICKY

Please. Come and sit down, Aleksi. (a joke, gestures) My "office."
You wanted to see me too.

Smiles to himself.

I was just thinking about our "home."

KARPOV

This [Lucia's house] does that.

He sits.

NICKY

What? Yes, it does, doesn't it? For me too. But I meant our "home"
now . . .Something Vera said.

Then:

I haven't congratulated you on your engagement. My first wife . . .

KARPOV (*nervous*)

You don't mind—?

NICKY

No. No. That was a long time ago. I'm happy she won't be alone. So
what can I do for you, my friend? Just say it. I am a friend . . .

Then:

KARPOV

I'm not a communist.

NICKY

That's good. That's very good. But why do you feel you have to tell
me that?

KARPOV

I teach piano.

NICKY

I know.

KARPOV

I'm Russian.

NICKY

Yes. I understand the distinction. I certainly do.

KARPOV

During the war, I was in Los Angeles, and a friend asked me to act a very small part in a film. I'm not even an actor.

Smiles.

An American film. A Hollywood film. I thought it would be fun. I think they liked my face.

NICKY

And was it? Fun.

KARPOV (*hesitates, then*)

Yes.

NICKY (*smiles*)

Good.

KARPOV

It was about the Soviets. Our allies—then. They were our allies.

NICKY

I know. I know.

KARPOV

So it praised the Soviets and Russians. How happy they are. How good their lives are. I only saw it once. It wasn't a very good picture.

NICKY

What's it called?

KARPOV

Song of Russia.

NICKY

Ah.

KARPOV

You know it.

NICKY

I know like everyone who listens to the radio knows that those who made this film are being . . .

KARPOV

I've been subpoenaed.

NICKY

I'm sorry. I'm very sorry.

KARPOV

I'm scared, Nicky.

NICKY

I'm sure you are . . .

KARPOV

What do they want from me?

NICKY

I'll make calls. I have some people I can call, Aleksi.

Then:

So how can you help them? That's what they're going to ask me.
When I make the calls.

KARPOV

But that's what I don't know, Nicky. Help them do what? What do
they want me to help them do?

NICKY

I think . . .

KARPOV

What?

NICKY

I think that they'd be interested to know in advance of your talking
to them, Aleksi—that you are ready and even eager—it's important
to them, I think, to be eager—to answer all of their questions. Of
course, that's correct, isn't it?

Then:

Isn't it? Are you eager?

KARPOV

Of course.

NICKY

Good. Then I can't see there'll be a problem. They appreciate
"eager" people.

> *Off,* KOLYA *has begun to play on the piano the Russian
> folk song, "Down the Peterskaya Road."* NICKY *recognizes
> the music and laughs.*

KARPOV

What?

NICKY

Igor used this melody in *Petrushka*. (*laughing*) For—"The Dance of
the Wet Nurses."

Then:
I'll make calls. Are we done?
        NICKY *stands.*
        *Off, some have begun to sing "Down the Peterskaya
        Road."*
They're singing now . . .

KARPOV

Thank you, Nicky. Thank you.
        Shakes his hand.
Natasha hasn't been sleeping because of this.
        As they head inside:

NICKY

So she asked you to ask me?

KARPOV

Where could I go?

NICKY

I'm just happy I can help. Both you and Natasha.
        IGOR *appears in the doorway. The singing, the party off
        continues.*

IGOR

Nicky . . . (*sees* KARPOV) I'm sorry, I'm interrupting.

NICKY

No, no. We're done. (*to* KARPOV) Aren't we done?

KARPOV

Yes. We are. Nicky—thank you.
        He hurries inside.

NICKY

I feel like I'm missing all the fun . . .
        IGOR *doesn't move.*
        Then:
Did you want to—talk, Igor?
        Then:
What, Igor?

IGOR

You need help—ask Nicky. We were just saying this.

Smiles.

What would we do without our Nicky?

Then:

Thank you. God bless you.

He holds him.

Vera hasn't been sleeping.

VERA *appears in the door.*

IGOR

VERA

Igor, Nicky come inside and join the party!

They put their arms around each other.

Crowd is singing.

IGOR

Come on, Nicky!

NICKY

Maybe I'll play you some jazz!

**A burst of laughter as the singing continues. They
go inside and join VERA and the party.**

Lights fade.

**MARIA and NICHOLAS, now in rehearsal clothes,
enter and begin to warm up. She is in a white tunic,
and white scarf—very Russian.**

**The scene behind them changes, and we are now
outside the barn, its doors wide open—inside has
been converted into a dance studio. Piano, etc.**

Scene Three

The Barn. Late evening.

Some lights are on and candles lit.

Everyone—NICKY, LUCIA, VERA, ANNA, SUDEIKIN, EVGENIA, NATALIA, NATASHA, KARPOV, LISA *and* VLADIMIR *are organizing chairs or a bench, etc—which thy have carried with them from the house—to watch the rehearsal. They are just outside the barn, looking in through the open doors.*

MARIA *and* NICHOLAS *are talking quietly.* GEORGE *and* IGOR—*who has seen nothing of the ballet as yet—stand waiting to one side.* KOLYA *opens the piano and plays a few notes.*

The "audience" is down stage, facing up.

LUCIA (*shouts to* KOLYA *in the barn*)
I had it tuned yesterday.

As the "audience" organizes itself:

ANNA
Mr. Sokoloff, what was the play you were just in?

LISA (*answering for him*)
Crime and Punishment.

KARPOV (*to* VLADIMIR)
Raskolnikoff?

VLADIMIR
That was Gielgud.

LUCIA
Oh—he's very Russian!

Laughter.

NATALIA
Mr. Sudeikin, why don't you sit here?

She has set a chair—in the middle, a place of honor.

LISA (*continuing the other conversation*)
My husband was the examining magistrate.

EVGENIA

That's a good part.

SUDEIKIN

And it's closed?

VLADIMIR

Gielgud was furious. He blamed the audience. He said they just don't understand Russians here!

LUCIA

Gielgud said this?

SUDEIKIN

Is he speaking for us now?

VLADIMIR

Americans, he said—are embarrassed by grown men beating their breasts.

NATALIA

But he's so—English.

LISA (*to* NATALIA)

That's what we're saying.

Still gossiping, waiting, getting organized:

SUDEIKIN (*to* VLADIMIR)

Is that the play Kimisarjevsky was doing?

VLADIMIR *nods.*

(*smiling*) You must have stories.

LISA (*for her husband*)

He's a good director.

SUDEIKIN (*to the others*)

He just keeps going and going. I give him that.

KOLYA *is practicing a few tricky bars.*

LISA

He's also doing *Andrea Chenier* at George's theater.

NATASHA

What theater's that?

LUCIA

He means City Center.

IGOR *has joined this group:*

IGOR

The pit there smells like a toilet.

VERA

You've told us this, Igor. Should we be quiet?

IGOR (*about* GEORGE *and the dancers*)

They're talking.

ANNA

Who's doing the dances for *Andrea Chenier*?

VLADIMIR

I don't know—.

LISA

William Dollar.

This gets a reaction from the group—"ohhhh."
One of George's dancers . . .

SUDEIKIN (*shouts*)

George!

GEORGE *turns.*

William Dollar! How good are his dances?

GEORGE (*as a reflex*)

They're getting better.

He goes back to talking to MARIA *and* NICHOLAS.

MARIA

What did he ask?

GEORGE

<u>Nothing.</u>

MARIA

He said something about William—.

GEORGE

Sh-sh.

SUDEIKIN (*smiling, up to mischief*)

George, *The Times* seems to like William Dollar's dances, doesn't he?

No one takes the bait.

LUCIA (*to* ANNA *who is confused*)

The Times dance critic.

SUDEIKIN

That man's a terrible human being. Awful critic.

LUCIA

We know . . .

SUDEIKIN (*to* ANNA)

The Times keeps saying George isn't "American enough." So—now look how George dresses. Those ties.

Gestures: the string tie.

LISA

Why *is* he wearing those?

NATASHA

He likes them.

SUDEIKIN

He's trying too hard. Next—it'll be a cowboy hat.

Turns to IGOR.

Igor, why are you making fun of Hans Eisler?

IGOR

I wasn't making—.

SUDEIKIN

I just heard you. Walking out here? I thought you liked his music.

To the others.

I hear he's being deported.

GEORGE *comes to join them.*

GEORGE

Igor, sit on the side—so we can talk.

SUDEIKIN

So—this ballet you're doing—it's going to be a big hit? You'll make a lot of money? Like your musicals, George.

He smiles.

GEORGE

Of course. I think Lincoln is hoping for at least 35% audience for both Monday *and* Tuesday nights!

Laughter.

Until now they've played to 30%.

LUCIA

Kirstein's just fired his manager.

SUDEIKIN

Shoot the messenger.

NATASHA

George always wants his ballets to be hits. He says—if people don't come, then the dancers can't get paid. And if the dancers can't get paid, they won't be able to eat. But it's only when they are able to eat that he can tell them—don't eat, get thin, do this, put on some make-up, you look like hell!

Laughter.

GEORGE (*about* NATASHA)

Someone who understands me.

Then:

We'll jump around in the story a little.

SUDEIKIN

And Igor you've seen nothing.

IGOR

No.

GEORGE

I will have a few questions for him.

To IGOR:

We'll start with Eurydice's Variation.

To MARIA:

Your variation, dear.

To LUCIA:

Lucia, explain to Sergey what we've been doing.

As LUCIA *explains,* GEORGE *fixes* MARIA's *scarf, checks out her toe shoes, etc.*

LUCIA (*to* SUDEIKIN)

This is when we first meet Eurydice in Hades. The beginning is soft, can barely be heard. Then she turns and starts walking toward Orpheus, then the music shifts.

Then:

He has her doing almost jazz steps. Very—Fred Astaire. Tap.

GEORGE

Kolya, show Mr. Stravinsky our tempo.

KOLYA *plays a bit and stops.*

IGOR

Fine. Good.

GEORGE (*to* MARIA)

Let us show Mr. Stravinsky what we've been doing and hopefully he will not hate it.

> GEORGE *places* MARIA *and goes and stands by* IGOR.

Kolya.

> KOLYA *begins to play.*

> *She dances the whole, wonderful variation, which lasts a little more than a minute and a half. It is sexy, witty, very modern, yet also somehow classical.*

> *As she dances once or twice he calls out a note to her:*

GEORGE

Maria, look at feet.

> *Then:*

Think, look at my beautiful feet.

> *She finishes.*

> *As she stops,* GEORGE *turns to* IGOR:

(*the point where the dance stopped*) Here. A few seconds. Here.

IGOR

"A few" isn't a number. How many?

GEORGE

Three.

IGOR

Three.

> IGOR *stands and heads for the piano.*

GEORGE (*surprised*)

You're going to do it now?

> *To* MARIA:

He's going to do it now.

> *Then, to* IGOR:

Do you want some time?

> *No response.*

> IGOR *and* KOLYA *begin to work out the change. Throughout the following* KOLYA *plays phrases for* IGOR.

Everyone has suddenly relaxed. They whisper among
themselves thrilled by what they have just seen.

    As he waits for IGOR:

(*to* MARIA) <u>Notes . . . In "walks."</u>

    He demonstrates, she follows.

<u>Elbows against sides . . . Strong spine . . . Dear, palms in . . .</u>

    He nods. She stops.

    He looks to IGOR.

Igor?

    No response as IGOR *works.*

(*to the group, smiling*) We have inspired him.

    Light laughter.

    He turns back to MARIA.

(*as he demonstrates*) <u>"Hand"</u> . . .

    Then another step.

<u>Here too</u> . . .

    The group strain to hear what he is saying to her.

    Another note:

(*to* MARIA) <u>"Going back." Tempo rushed.</u>

    He sings a line. He stops her.

<u>Dear, Mr. Stravinsky is a patient man. No reason to hurry.</u>

    The group laughs a little at this.

    After another look at IGOR:

<u>Let's see</u> . . .

    She continues as he sings.

    He stops her.

    Another look at IGOR, KOLYA *and* IGOR *are still working,*

    GEORGE *gets* NICHOLAS:

<u>In the pas de deux. From "searching."</u>

    As MARIA *and* NICHOLAS *do a movement.*

<u>You are saying—no I can't look.</u> (*to* MARIA) <u>And you are saying—look.</u>
<u>Better.</u> (*to* MARIA) <u>You initiate. Again.</u>

    As they do the movement again.

<u>She is yours—as long as you don't look. But it hurts you very much not</u>
<u>to see her . . . You want him to look and see this beauty. Yes. Now lift.</u>

    He demonstrates.

You search for her hands because you can't see . . .
        NICHOLAS *steps in.*
Try.
        As NICHOLAS *does the lift:*

IGOR
(*interrupting, having finished his correction*) All right. Go on.
        Then about the change:
I've made you happy.

GEORGE (*to* IGOR)
Don't you want to sit back—[here]?

IGOR
I'm fine here.

VERA (*making a joke, calls*)
He likes to be on the stage.
        Laughter.

GEORGE (*to* IGOR)
We don't have a mask. We'll mime the mask.

IGOR
But he will look like a baseball catcher?

GEORGE
Of course.

IGOR
Good.

GEORGE (*to* LUCIA)
The Pas de Deux.

        GEORGE *positions* NICHOLAS *and* MARIA.

VERA (*about* NICHOLAS, *to* SUDEIKIN)
He's a beautiful boy.

SUDEIKIN
He is.

GEORGE
Lucia . . .

LUCIA
(*explaining to* SUDEIKIN, *as the whole group listens*) The Pas de
Deux. As Orpheus and Eurydice head to earth, she tries to get him
to look at her . . . If he looks at her she dies . . .

GEORGE

Kolya.

> *Nods to* KOLYA, KOLYA *plays and we watch* NICHOLAS
> *and* MARIA *do the pas de deux—over three minutes—*
> *the dance is a beautiful and very sexual pas de deux.*

> *Two or three times* GEORGE *calls out a note:*

GEORGE

Touch him, Maria.
> *Another.*
Don't look . . .
> *Another.*
She's yours if you don't look . . .
> *And the dance ends with Orpheus suddenly pulling off*
> *his mask and Eurydice dying. She dies.*

> *In a flash* GEORGE *is at* IGOR's *side, and they are talking*
> *—we can't understand what they are saying.*

> *The guests murmur among themselves, thrilled by this*
> *as well.* ANNA *is overwhelmed.*

LUCIA

Niece, are you all right?

ANNA

It's so beautiful, Aunt Lucia. I can't believe how beautiful. She is . . .

LUCIA (*hugs her*)

It is very beautiful.
> *Then,* IGOR *turns to* MARIA:

IGOR (*in English*)

Maria? How long it take you to die?
> *She doesn't know—she puts her head on* NICHOLAS's
> *shoulders and begins to fall to the floor—*IGOR *snaps his*
> *fingers—four times.*
That's enough. Now you are dead.
> *And he turns to make this correction in his score,* GEORGE
> *watching over his shoulder, at his side.*

VERA (*to* LUCIA)

Igor's very pleased.

VLADIMIR (*to* SUDEIKIN)
What do you think, Sergey?

SUDEIKIN
They should have asked me to design it . . .
When suddenly arriving out of the woods comes another
Russian guest, SERGE KOUSSEVITZKY.

KOUSSEVITZKY (*calls behind him*)
I found them!!

NATASHA
Maestro!

KOUSSEVITZKY
My god it's a theater.
Suddenly all react and stand:

KOLYA
Maestro . . .

LUCIA
Serge. I thought you weren't coming—.

NATASHA
Did you get lost?

LUCIA (*over this*)
Why didn't you telephone? We'd given up.

KOUSSEVITZKY (*joking*)
Should I go home?

LUCIA & NATASHA
No! No!
He greets LUCIA *and* NATASHA.

NICKY
I didn't realize you were coming—

NATASHA (*over the noise*)
Lucia wasn't sure if he could make it. (*to* KOUSSEVITZKY) Who don't
you know?
KOUSSEVITZKY *sees* SUDEIKIN:

KOUSSEVITZKY
Mr. Sudeikin! I believe this is in honor of you.
SUDEIKIN *slowly stands:*

SUDEIKIN

You're late.

KOUSSEVITZKY *smiles.*

KOUSSEVITZKY

Don't get up, my friend. Don't get up. (*to* GEORGE *and* IGOR) George, Igor, what have I interrupted? (*answering* NATASHA's question) I know everyone.

SUDEIKIN

I'm already up. Why didn't anyone tell me he was invited? I wouldn't have come.

The two men embrace.

So—maestro—have you learned to sight read yet?

Others are not sure if this is funny.

Then:

KOUSSEVITZKY

Have you learned to draw feet?

Laughter.

(*noticing* ANNA) You, I don't know you.

LUCIA

My niece. This is Mr. Koussevitzky, Anna.

KOUSSEVITZKY (*to* ANNA)

Stay away from the men, dear.

Others laugh.

I've interrupted something interesting. All of Russia seems to be hiding in these woods. What are we hiding from?

LUCIA

They're rehearsing.

KOUSSEVITZKY (*greeting*)

Nicky, how are you? I heard you would be here.

NICKY

Did you?

CHARLES "CHIP" BOHLEN (*42*) *enters from the shadows.*

KOUSSEVITZKY (*to* BOHLEN)

They're all Russian! It's only Russians! Will you forgive me?

He laughs, turns back:

(*to the others*) I brought along an American friend who is staying with me.

This quiets the others. IGOR *and* GEORGE *stop talking.*

(*to the others*) Careful what you say—he speaks perfect Russian. (*introducing*) Charles . . .

BOHLEN (*correcting him, smiling*)
"Chip." My friends call me.

KOUSSEVITZKY
"Chip"—for some reason he likes to be called "Chip."

BOHLEN
It's from college. (*recognizing each one*) Mr. Stravinsky, an honor. Mr. Balanchine. Mr. Sokoloff. Nicky Nabokov I know. We know each other, don't we, Nika?

He shakes their hands.

NATASHA
Your Russian is very good.

NICKY (*shaking his hand*)
Chip.

BOHLEN
Mr. Sudeikin . . .

KARPOV
You know your Russians.

KOUSSEVITZKY
His wife's called "Avis." What kind of name is that? Americans and their names.

CHIP *laughs.*

BOHLEN (*looking around*)
This feels like Russia. (*smiles*)

NICKY
Does it?

VERA (*leaning over to* KOUSSEVITZKY, *about* BOHLEN)
He speaks very good Russian.

KOUSSEVITZKY
Chip was with our embassy in Moscow. He lived there. For many years.

KOLYA *plays the cut measure or the musical change on
the piano for* IGOR *and* GEORGE.
The others quiet down.

LUCIA (*to* BOHLEN)

It's their new ballet.

KOUSSEVITZKY (*to* VERA *continuing about* BOHLEN)

He was the President's interpreter at Yalta . . .

LUCIA

Mr. Koussevitzky, sit.

NATASHA (*to* BOHLEN)

And—.

BOHLEN

I'm happy standing.

KOUSSEVITZKY

Now tell me, what have we interrupted?

VERA (*to* KOUSSEVITZKY)

Serge, sit—everyone. George is just showing Igor—.

KOUSSEVITZKY

I'll sit over there, out of the way.

VERA

Sit here. Sit.

NICKY (*to* BOHLEN)

Here take my seat . . .

BOHLEN

It's yours, Nika. I just want to be a fly on the wall. Ignore me . . .
Smiles.
GEORGE *and* IGOR *are still quietly talking at the piano.*
Short pause.

LUCIA

They're talking. So–shsh . . .
Short pause. All is quiet.

VERA (*leans over to* KOUSSEVITZKY)

So good to see you. (*leans over again*) I think Igor wants to talk to
you about something.
KOUSSEVITZKY *smiles but doesn't respond.*

NICKY (*surprised, to* VERA)

Vera, what about?

GEORGE *and* IGOR *finish talking.*

GEORGE (to LUCIA)

Next I'll show Igor the opening. *Nicholas . . .*

GEORGE *sets a coatrack to stand in for the grave.*

LUCIA

Shhhhh.

GEORGE

Kolya . . .

KOLYA

I heard . . .

LUCIA (*to everyone*)

Shhhh . . .

GEORGE *waits for the room to settle, then nods to* KOLYA.

KOLYA *starts to play the opening.*

They listen, then, as nothing seems to be happening, KOUSSEVITZKY *turns back to* CHIP.

KOUSSEVITZKY (*to* CHIP)

Chip, when Igor and Vera first came here, to live—

NATASHA (*to* KOUSSEVITZKY)

This is Igor's opening, Serge. Sh-sh . . .

The music plays, he listens, then:

KOUSSEVITZKY (*to* CHIP)

I was Igor and Vera's only friend who would let them sleep in the same room.

Smiles at VERA.

In the same bed!

Smiles.

They weren't married yet. I kept asking Vera are you really divorced? For Christ's sake, enjoy yourself—

LUCIA

Serge . . .

KOUSSEVITZKY

(*finishing his story, to* CHIP)—enjoy, yourself, I said (*turns to* VERA) you have been through so much.

BOHLEN (*surprising everyone*)

Serge, please shut up.

Laughs. The room is suddenly quiet. KOLYA *stops playing.*

NICKY

Chip—.

CHIP

I think the artists want us to be quiet.

KOUSSEVITZKY (*to the shocked group*)

It's all right. He's right.

VERA(*to* BOHLEN)

This is Serge Koussevitzky . . .

KOUSSEVITZKY (*to* VERA)

He knows. It's fine.
    Then:
I interrupted. (*to* LUCIA) So that was the opening. Very nice, Igor . . .

LUCIA

Like a prelude. The curtain is still in.

BOHLEN (*to* NICKY)

Our curtain, Nika?

Everyone hears this.

NICKY

No. This is the theater curtain.

BOHLEN

Where's our curtain?

NICKY

It comes in later.

BOHLEN (*to the others*)

I hear it's beautiful. It should be, it cost enough. (*smiles*)

LUCIA *now turns and explains to* BOHLEN:

LUCIA

The first scene is at the grave of Orpheus's wife.

NATASHA (*pointing to* BOHLEN)

The coat rack's the grave, Mr. Bohlen.

BOHLEN

I understand. I've been to rehearsals once or twice before. (*smiles*)

LISA

Have you.

LUCIA

Orpheus will play his lyre.

BOHLEN

That's what that is . . .

LUCIA

And as he plays he remembers how he and his wife used to dance together. So he remembers and he dances . . . That's the first scene.

BOHLEN

Thank you. It all sounds so interesting.

GEORGE

Mr. Bohlen, may we continue?

BOHLEN

You weren't waiting for me?

GEORGE

Igor, where from?

BOHLEN (*to* NICKY)

Why were they waiting for me?

IGOR (*to* GEORGE)

The curtain going up . . .?

GEORGE *takes* NICHOLAS *to his place at the grave.*

GEORGE

Kolya . . . Just before curtain.

Music starts again. Music plays, then:

Curtain.

LUCIA (*to* BOHLEN)

Friends will walk by. But Orpheus doesn't even see them.

We hear the music for this.

GEORGE

(*to* IGOR, *showing the beat the friends enter on*) That's one girl. She has the mask. The boy, he brings the pole. (*listens, then:*) Other girl, with the shawl.

BOHLEN (*to* LUCIA)

What's he saying?

LUCIA

He's talking to Igor. They're working.

VERA

He's not talking to us.

GEORGE *walks this, mimes this:*

GEORGE

The pole . . . The mask . . . Puts on the shawl . . . Put hand on his shoulder . . . and walk off.

GEORGE *walks off.*

NICKY (*to* BOHLEN)

Sit. Sit down. Take my chair.

LUCIA

No, sit here. Take mine . . .

BOHLEN *takes his seat beside* SUDEIKIN.

BOHLEN (*smiles to* SUDEIKIN, *as a joke*)

We've got the best seats.

Pats SUDEIKIN *on the knee.*

LUCIA (*offering a seat*)

Nicky . . .

NICKY

I'm fine.

NICHOLAS *nods to* KOLYA *who plays and* NICHOLAS *dances the opening.*

He finishes; the crowd stirs; NICHOLAS *breathes heavily.*

GEORGE *looks at* IGOR *at the piano.*

Out of the silence, and the breathing:

BOHLEN

Nicky, all this in the middle of the woods. In—Connecticut.

Lights fade.

Scene Four

The study of the house. A sofa, chairs, a bar set up on a desk, and a piano.

Later that night, around midnight. Only a couple of lights are on. Off, fireworks, celebrating SUDEIKIN. *We can see the shadows of people on the porch. Laughter from the porch.*

NICKY *sits by the record player, looking through records, and listening to a popular Russian folk song, "Birch Trees."*

KOLYA *enters and goes to the "bar."*

ANNA *sits at the window, watching something or someone out on the porch.*

Fireworks in the distance.

After a look at NICKY, *as* KOLYA *pours himself a drink:*

> NICKY

I think Igor's already stolen all the good Russian folk songs. And what he didn't steal, others before him did.
> *Laughs to himself.*

Tchaikovsky used this in his 4th—. (*as a joke*) What's left for me?
> *Laughs.*

> KOLYA

Are you still writing music, Nicky?

> NICKY

I'm a composer.
> *He takes off the record.*

Why did you ask that?

> KOLYA

I was under the impression you'd stopped. Too busy.

> NICKY

Did George say that?

KOLYA

I guess I was misinformed, Nicky.

Fireworks off.

We're missing Aleksi's fireworks.

NICKY *puts on a second record: M. Smirnov's choral piece, sung by a female chorus, "Dear Birch-tree." It is slow and reflective.*

NICKY (*as he listens*)

I'm always trying to write, Kolya. That's a curse sometimes, isn't it?

Smiles.

Actually, I was just thinking—I can't wait to get back to my piano. I think I've been inspired. (*smiles*) The dance is very very good isn't it? Funny, I had a feeling I haven't had for a long time—that maybe this is how it used to be? This feeling. Or am I just being sentimental?

Looks up at KOLYA.

Well if it's not how it was, it's how it should have been.

Then about Orpheus:

Igor's music is not simple. It's got me thinking . . . The competitive juices are flowing . . .

He smiles.

NATALIA *appears in the doorway.*

NATALIA (*to* NICKY)

We're going to put food out on the porch, Nicky.

To KOLYA:

How's your Uncle?

KOLYA

Awake, barely. A long day. A good day. And, I think, he's happy . . .

NATALIA

He deserves that.

Sees ANNA:

Anna? Can you help? (*to* NICKY) I'll call you when the food's been set out.

KOLYA

My Uncle told me walking back from the barn—"Kolya, I guess I'm not forgotten."

GEORGE *enters.*

NICKY

Tell George that, he'll be pleased.

NATALIA

George, we're eating outside.

She notices GEORGE *and* ANNA *looking at each other.*

Anna, are you going to help?

NICKY *seeing* GEORGE, *stops the record.*

GEORGE

I'll send her right out, Natalia.

NATALIA *hesitates and then leaves.*

NICKY *watches, while continuing to look at records.* KOLYA
tries not to watch.

NICKY (*to* GEORGE)

Kolya was just saying Sergey—.

GEORGE (*his thoughts on* ANNA, *to* ANNA)

Now what is so important it can't wait?

She just looks at him.

Can't you speak?

She smiles and shakes her head.

GEORGE *smiles, looks at* NICKY.

KOLYA *looks down or away.*

(*to* NICKY) She's been tapping on that window and telling me to come
in for the last twenty minutes.

Then:

Anna, I'm going back outside now.

He turns to go.

ANNA

I want to be a dancer.

Then:

I am a dancer.

GEORGE

What do you think that means?

No response.

NICKY

I've heard you say—.

GEORGE

Be quiet. I'm talking to her. (*shaking his head, then to* NICKY) She wants
to be a dancer. How many times a day do I hear someone say that?

> *Then to* ANNA:

Point your feet. Plié. (*She does*) Let me see your legs, Anna.

> *She lifts up her skirt a little.*

Your legs . . . Your bottom. Lift up your dress.

> *She does.*

> MARIA *appears in the doorway.* NICKY *sees her,* GEORGE
> *doesn't.* MARIA *watches* GEORGE *with* ANNA.

NICKY (*about* MARIA)

Kolya . . .

> KOLYA *seeing* MARIA, *purposefully looks away, out the*
> *window, sipping his drink.*

GEORGE

Higher.

NICKY (*warning about* MARIA)

George . . .

> ANNA *raises her skirt higher.* GEORGE *shares a look with*
> NICKY, *doesn't see* MARIA.

GEORGE (*to* ANNA)

Thank you.

ANNA

Can I put my dress down now?

> *No response. She continues to hold it up.*

> NICKY *watches* MARIA *leave,* GEORGE *hasn't seen her.*

GEORGE (*then*)

How old are you Anna?

ANNA (*ignoring the question*)

I'd like to be you.

GEORGE

What??

> *He turns to* NICKY, *confused.*

What is she talking about?

ANNA

And feel what it's like to be famous and talented. To feel what fame is like. What does it feel like?

GEORGE, *confused, then suddenly the "penny drops" and he laughs.*

GEORGE

And you are a seagull. I get it.

ANNA

What??

GEORGE

You're quoting from the play.

ANNA

What play?

GEORGE

The Seagull. Chekhov.

ANNA

I don't know that play.

GEORGE

You don't? You were saying her lines—?

ANNA

What happens in this play?

GEORGE (*hesitates, then after a look at* NICKY)

There's a famous writer. And there's this young girl. And she wants to be famous. And wants to know what it's like and . . .

ANNA

Just like me. And what does he say? The famous writer.

GEORGE

He says—it's boring, hard work. He's always thinking about his work. You don't know it?

She shakes her head, then:

ANNA

And then what happens to her?

GEORGE *takes another look back at* NICKY, *then:*

GEORGE

She—.

ANNA (*before he can answer*)
Does she go to another town, have his child, and go crazy?

He suddenly realizes he's been tricked:

GEORGE
You know it! You little—. You—. She lied! You lied!

She runs out of the room, laughing.

To NICKY:

She tricked me, Nicky. She's a teenager and she tricks me. You'd think I'd learn. I am such a sucker. These girls are worse than the women . . .

VLADIMIR (*in the doorway, calls back*)
Here he is! He's in here with Nicky!

A crowd, led by VLADIMIR *comes to the doorway, it includes* KOUSSEVITZKY, LISA, VERA, LUCIA, NATASHA, NATALIA *and in the back,* ANNA. VLADIMIR *has a plate of food.*

GEORGE
What is this—?

VLADIMIR
George, we've come to talk to you.

KOUSSEVITZKY
I had no idea he was so ill. It just breaks my heart to look at him. But this is a good thing you all are doing.

GEORGE
Is Sergey all right?

LUCIA
He's asleep. At the table. On the porch. His head on the . . .

VLADIMIR (*offering to* GEORGE)
Would you like something to eat?

GEORGE
I'm fine. I've eaten enough. What is this about? What do you want?

NICKY
Where's Igor?

VERA
He's still on the porch talking with the American.

NICKY

What are they talking about?

VLADIMIR

I heard him ask Igor what American composers he admired.

GEORGE

That's not a long conversation.

VLADIMIR (*to the others*)

Should I be the one—?

To GEORGE.

We have an idea. To do something nice—for Sudeikin. He was—just a few minutes ago—he started to talk about your Orpheus, George. Not the ballet. The boy. About—him being such a beautiful boy. You should have seen how his face lit up.

Turns to others.

KOUSSEVITZKY

It was like he suddenly wasn't sick. While he talked about this boy.

LUCIA

We all noticed this.

VLADIMIR

So we thought maybe tonight this boy . . .?

KOLYA

Nicholas.

GEORGE

What?

VLADIMIR

Nicholas. What if he stayed with Sudeikin. Just in the room. Just sit on a chair, even sleep on the sofa. So when Sergey woke, he could see him. We're not saying he should even get undressed. Probably better if he didn't.

Others nod.

Then:

This was Vera's idea.

GEORGE *looks to* VERA.

VERA

He likes to look. He always liked to look—at something beautiful.

Then:

GEORGE

Why are you asking me?

VLADIMIR

He's your dancer. He's here because of you. We—.

GEORGE

Ask him. Tell him why. See what he says.

VLADIMIR

Are you sure?
    Then:
(*to the others*) Do we know where the boy is?

KOLYA

I think he's still in the barn. Working.

VERA (*hurrying out*)

I'll go ask him.

LISA

You want me to go with you?
    She is already gone.
She's already gone . . .

    They wait.

    From outside on the porch, BOHLEN *and* IGOR *burst out
    laughing.*

LISA (*about the laughter, to* VLADIMIR)

Chip . . .

NICKY

Igor's found an audience.
    Then:

ANNA

Aunt Lucia, what are we doing?

LUCIA

We're waiting . . .

GEORGE

Lucia, your niece tells me she's a dancer.
    Everyone looks at ANNA.

LUCIA

Anna, have you been—[bothering]?

GEORGE

I should like to work with her a while—and see.

LISA

Where's Maria?

NICKY

I'm guessing—she went to bed.

LUCIA

She told me she was tired. I suppose with everyone speaking Russian . . .

ANNA

That must be hard.

KOLYA (*nods*)

She went to bed.

> *Then to change the subject:*

GEORGE

I think this is a good idea. I do. (*then*) Asking Nicholas. If he says he doesn't want to . . . We'll see . . .

> *Then:*

LUCIA

He was going to sleep on some couch anyway . . .

> *Short pause as they wait.*

KOUSSEVITZKY (*to* VLADIMIR, *to say something*)

Vladimir, I am sorry I missed your *Crime and Punishment*.

VLADIMIR

You're not the only one. No one came.

KOUSSEVITZKY

I heard it was very good.

GEORGE

At least he got to use his Russian accent for a change.

> *Others laugh.*

ANNA

What? What's funny?

LUCIA

Vladimir is the master of accents!

VLADIMIR (*to* ANNA)

And they all sound the same. But no one seems to care in the movies.

LUCIA

He's played—?

To VLADIMIR.

How many?

LISA (*answering for him*)

At least thirty-five.

LUCIA

Thirty-five different nationalities in the movies!

GEORGE

And all with the same accent!

Laughter.

VLADIMIR (*to* ANNA)

I've been:

He does an "accent" and gestures—always a stereotype —for each, and all sound similar:

A Greek villain: "You going to die, mister." A Filipino villain: "You going to die, mister." A Mexican villain: "You going to die, mister." Italian: "You going to die, mister." Turkish—.

Laughter.

LISA

A red Indian.

VLADIMIR

(*does his "American Indian" accent:*) Red Indian: "You going to—" *Stops.*

Maria isn't—?

GEORGE

I think she went to bed.

VLADIMIR (*to* NICKY)

You said. (*then, his "Indian"*) "You going to die—."

LUCIA (*looking out onto the porch*)

Here they come.

LISA

Does the boy look like he agreed? Is he going to do it?

LUCIA

I can't tell . . .

> *They all look to the doorway.*

> VERA *and* NICHOLAS *come in.*

VERA *(entering, to* LUCIA*)*

There's a sofa in Sergey's bedroom?

LUCIA

There is.

VERA

He seems fine with this. I think he understands.

NATALIA

(to NICHOLAS, *in English, but speaking as if he were deaf)* He likes to look at beautiful things.

NATASHA

He's not deaf, Natalia.

VLADIMIR

Should we go outside, wake him up and tell him?

KOUSSEVITZKY

Let's go . . . Quietly.

LUCIA

Quietly . . .

VLADIMIR

I want to see his face . . .

> *The crowd starts to go outside.*

GEORGE

Nicholas . . .

> *They stop.*

Thank you. Thank you. It will make an old man happy.

LISA

(putting her arm around Nicholas) You were very good this evening. Wasn't he?

> *The others quickly agree.*

He was very good.

> GEORGE *and* NICKY *stay back.* KOLYA *remains in his seat.* ANNA *goes to the window and "looks off."* NATASHA *also stays behind.*

GEORGE (*stopping her*)
Vera. Is he really all right about this?

VERA
He said as long as there's a sofa—he doesn't care who watches him sleep.

GEORGE
Did you offer him money?

VERA
Of course.

GEORGE *begins to follow* VERA.

ANNA
Mr. Balanchine . . .?

After a look at ANNA, VERA *goes out.*
The crowd is gone. GEORGE *has stopped and looks at* ANNA.
It's a wonderful thing to do. I think the only thing any of us ever really wants—is to see beauty. Or be a part of something that is beautiful.

She looks at GEORGE, *smiling; as she heads out and he follows:*
I look forward to your working with me, Mr. Balanchine.

ANNA *and* GEORGE *are gone.*

Burst of laughter and cheers from the porch. SUDEIKIN *has been woken and is being told of his surprise.*

NICKY *starts to follow* GEORGE.

NICKY (*to* NATASHA)
Aren't you going to watch?

NATASHA *looks at* KOLYA, *who looks at* NICKY.
What? What do you want? I've closed up shop for the night. Even the Voice of America needs to rest its voice sometimes. (*smiles*)

KOLYA (*pushing ahead, playing with his drink*)
George was earlier telling us a story about when he was a student in St. Petersburg. And how on certain days the security officers—the Cheka?

NICKY
I know what the Cheka is.

NATASHA *says nothing.*

KOLYA (*continues*)
And these officers were allowed to come to the rehearsals. And how

they'd line the wall and watch the girls stretch. Bend over. Lift their legs onto the bar.

Sips.

And how the school got money for this. And how, he said, every so often during one of these visits, a girl would be pointed out, she'd leave class—with an officer; and be gone for the rest of the day.

Laughter off.

Then my Uncle—he said something very interesting. He said—to Mr.—.

NATASHA

To "Chip."

NICKY *just looks at her.*

Mr. Bohlen was out there. When he was telling the story.

KOLYA

To "Chip"—that he'd read somewhere some rich son of a bitch saying that without Popes and millionaires there'd never have been any art in the world . . . But for them . . .

Then:

What my Uncle was saying, I think, is that in some people's eyes, the artist doesn't really matter—.

NICKY

I understood.

KOLYA

What matters is who pays.

NICKY

I said, I understood, Kolya.

Then:

KOLYA

And what that rich person wants. He gets.

NICKY *(then)*

And what did Chip Bohlen say to that? If he said anything?

KOLYA

That he wasn't a Catholic and wasn't a millionaire, that he just worked for the United States government—so he wouldn't know.

Then:

My Uncle then said, what the hell—he's going to say what he damn well wants now. He said to "Chip": "'Chip,' you know, some people think when they pay for art, they've also bought the artist."

Then:

> NICKY

And "Chip" said . . .?

> KOLYA

That with some artists—that was in fact true.

> *Then:*

> NICKY

And just why are you saying this to me? (*to both of them*) I don't want him here either. I didn't invite him.

> KOLYA

He's your friend. George says he's your friend.

> NICKY

George said that?

> KOLYA

I've known George a long long time, Nika. I've seen the good and the bad. (*looks to* NATASHA) We all have. Sure, I get frustrated with him. Even bored. I've heard the stories again and again. And when his mother died, I had to write the letters to his family. He just signed them. He should be better than that.

> *Then:*

But then I sit at the piano, and I watch him . . . Make something . . . You watched tonight.

> NICKY

I watched tonight.

> KOLYA

Leave him alone, Nicky.

> NICKY (*stunned*)

What am I—?

> KOLYA

Leave them alone. And tell that to your friends.

> KOLYA *stands.*

> NICKY

What the hell are you talking about? (*to* NATASHA) Does this make sense to you? (*no response, to* KOLYA) I'm not like Bohlen. I'm not fighting any war! I just want to help. I'm Russian.

KOLYA

And don't forget that, Nicky.

NICKY

I just want to help! I'm helping!

KOLYA *goes.*

(*shouts*) For Christ's sake, I paid for his damn curtain! You son of a bitch. Who does he think he is?!

NATASHA

You're shouting, Nicky. They can hear . . .

Short pause.

NICKY (*quietly*)

He's a fucking rehearsal piano player. He can't understand . . .

NATASHA

What's to understand, Nika?

Then:

He's just trying to protect George.

NICKY (*smiling, a joke*)

From me?

No response.

NATASHA

He shouldn't be hanging around Bohlen.

NICKY

George is a big boy. He can take care of himself. You know, I can't imagine what it must be like for you two. You and Lucia.

NATASHA

Nicky—.

NICKY

To be in love with George. And yet there you are having to watch him with others—even procure them for him.

NATASHA

Why are you being so mean?

Then:

Just keep Mr. Bohlen away from George.

NICKY

Haven't I already done you a favor today?

Then:

NATASHA

Thank you for your help with Aleksi. He was very worried. Thank you, Nicky.

NICKY

Karpov's a very stupid man. What do you think you're doing? Is this some way to punish yourself? If you can't have George, then . . .

NATASHA

Why are you saying this to me?!

NICKY

It's what it looks like. Just grab the first Russian—?
     Laughter off.
You deserve better.

NATASHA

You, I suppose?

NICKY

Better than me. Much better than me.

NATASHA

That doesn't eliminate many, Nicky.
     Then:
We do what we have to do. Don't we, Nicky? You certainly must understand that . . .

NICKY

What do you mean by that?

     VERA, SUDEIKIN *and* KOLYA *enter on their way, taking* SUDEIKIN *and* NICHOLAS *upstairs.*

     LUCIA (*to* SUDEIKIN, *to say something*)
Did you like the fireworks?

SUDEIKIN

What??

VERA

We had fireworks.

NATASHA (*to* SUDEIKIN)
They were nice.

SUDEIKIN (*to* NICHOLAS)
I used to paint a rose on Salome's knee every night.

KOLYA

He doesn't speak Russian.

> LUCIA, LISA, VLADIMIR, NATALIA *and* LUCIA *enter behind them.*

NATASHA

You're all going up?

KOLYA

There is no couch in my Uncle's room.

LUCIA

I'd moved it. I forgot.

VLADIMIR

We're moving one back . . .

> VLADIMIR *and* KOLYA *head off upstairs.*

LUCIA

We're getting him sheets.

NATASHA (*to* LISA)

And a blanket . . .

LUCIA (*going off with* LISA)

We'll take them off my bed . . .

> *They wait as* SUDEIKIN *makes his slow way across the room.* NATALIA *has gone off into the kitchen*

VERA

Nicholas—and you are sure this is fine?

KOLYA

I'm just sleeping on a couch, right?

VERA

That is right.

NICHOLAS

By myself . . .

VERA

By yourself . . .

KOLYA

Sure.

SUDEIKIN (*to* NICHOLAS)

I move very slowly. I'm sorry, young man.

VERA

He doesn't speak Russian, Sergey . . .

They are off.

KARPOV *at the door. He has watched* SERGEY *and* NICHOLAS.

KARPOV

He seems happy.

They turn to him.

There are some fireworks left. What should I do with them? I only used maybe half . . .

NATASHA

Ask Evgenia or Natalia. They're probably in the kitchen. I'll be right there . . .

KARPOV

And you liked them? The fireworks.

NATASHA

We all did, Aleksi. It was a very nice idea. Sergey loved them. I'll be right there . . .

KARPOV *goes to the kitchen.*

Then:

NICKY

What did you mean—we do what we have to do? Why say that to me?

NATASHA

Vera was saying in the kitchen earlier . . .

NICKY

What? What was she saying?

NATASHA

What if there's a revolution in *this* country? Where do we go? Who wants us? We're all scared.

NICKY

But this is America, Natasha. There's not going to be a revolution here.

NATASHA

What if one day they just decide they don't like us? What then?!

NICKY (*over the end of this*)
They're not going to throw us out!

NATASHA
Did your "Chip" promise you that?

NICKY
He's not "my"—.
    KOUSSEVITZKY *is in the doorway.*

KOUSSEVITZKY
Is this a private conversation?
    NATASHA *gets up and heads for the door.*

NATASHA
Come in, maestro. I was just leaving. (*to* NICKY) You should get married again, Nicky. It's too hard being alone.
    She hurries off to the kitchen.
(*calls*) Aleksi!

NICKY
How could she even think of marrying that man?

KOUSSEVITZKY (*pouring himself a drink*)
We do what we have to do.

NICKY
Natasha just said the same thing . . .

KOUSSEVITZKY
You're not going upstairs to see—.

NICKY
No. It's a very nice thing to do for Sergey, though.

KOUSSEVITZKY (*as he pours himself a drink*)
I saw you in here, Nicky. I said to myself, I'm not going to let this weekend go by without talking to Nicky.

NICKY
It's good to see you too, Serge.

KOUSSEVITZKY
Tell me—what are you writing? I wanted to ask.
    Surprised, NICKY *looks at him.*
It's been a while. I know. I know it's hard. Believe me, I know. But we need to fight for the time. Make the time, if you don't . . . No one just gives it to us. I'm very much looking forward to your next piece.

NICKY

Thank you, maestro. I appreciate that. I really do.

KOUSSEVITZKY

For orchestra or—chamber?

NICKY

I'm thinking chamber.

KOUSSEVITZKY

That's—practical. Good for you. It's been a while. So it's smart to be practical. You haven't been to Tanglewood in ages, Nicky. You should come—it's inspiring.

NICKY

I've been. I know.

KOUSSEVITZKY

Now's my favorite time there—hardly anyone around. We're still planning the summer. I'm left alone. Though friends are always coming through—Tanglewood—.

NICKY

Like Chip?

KOUSSEVITZKY

He was visiting. I didn't think I could even come. Then something got cancelled. I couldn't just leave him.

NICKY *looks at* KOUSSEVITZKY.

He's our friend. I wanted to see Sudeikin. A great man. In his time. An artist. No, I meant the Russians who come through Tanglewood, Boston . . . For some unknown reason, more and more they talk about—going back to—Europe now. Rome. Paris. And leave this "godforsaken place." What are they talking about, Nicky?

Then:

Tell me, is it true—George has been offered La Scala? Is he going to go?

NICKY

So this is about George.

KOUSSEVITZKY

Is it true? Chip wanted to know. George never tells me anything.

NICKY

You want to talk about George.

KOUSSEVITZKY

Europe is awful. That's what I tell my Russian friends. People there die in the street. And people walk right by; they are that used to it there. Little boys and girls sell themselves for candy bars. This is where we now belong. We both know this. We were all happy when George had come back from Paris. We need him—here.

Then:

We understand that, don't we? You bought George a curtain.

NICKY

Did he tell you that?

KOUSSEVITZKY

No, Chip did. He watches very closely how his money gets spent. Believe me, I know. Keep receipts.

Laughs.

Igor looks good. Vera makes him human. Everyone needs money. Everyone needs help. Kirstein's looking for money. Do you think they can help?

Then:

If it helps keep George here . . .

NICKY

This weekend is just for us, maestro. Russians.

KOUSSEVITZKY

Chip speaks Russian—. The dancers. George's wife—.

NICKY

They're dancers. Only Russians. In the woods for one goddamn weekend! To forget where we are.

KOUSSEVITZKY

Is that why we're here?

NATALIA, EVGENIA *and* NATASHA *come from the kitchen and pass through on their way to the porch.*

NATALIA

(to NICKY and KOUSSEVITZKY) It's gotten chilly, we're going to tell them that we'll set out the food in here.

As they head back off to the porch.

EVGENIA (*to* NATASHA)

Anna should be helping . . .

NATALIA

Where is Anna . . .?

They are gone.

KOUSSEVITZKY

Chip Bohlen's our friend, Nika . . .

VLADIMIR *and* LISA *enter from upstairs:*

VLADIMIR *(entering, to* LISA*)*

He sounded pleased . . . Didn't he?

LISA

I think he was. I think he was very pleased.

VLADIMIR

I think so too.

KARPOV *(entering from the kitchen)*

They're bringing the food into here. It's gotten cold . . .

VLADIMIR

I left the cards outside. We are still playing cards?

VERA *returns from upstairs, distracted.*

KARPOV

I'll play. I can play now. *(as he follows* VLADIMIR *out to get the cards)*
How did you like the fireworks?

They are gone.

LISA *(to* VERA*)*

I'm not playing cards with him.

NATALIA *and* EVGENIA *carry in a few glasses, etc. From
the porch to the kitchen.* NATASHA *is behind them.*

LUCIA *and* KOLYA *return from upstairs.*

NICKY *(to* VERA*)*

Is everything all right upstairs?

KOUSSEVITZKY

Was he pleased?

VERA

We think he's happy . . . *(to* LISA*)* Don't we?

LISA

Yes. He's happy.

VERA

I think we did the right thing.

> VLADIMIR *and* KARPOV *have returned with the cards.*

KARPOV (*at the piano*)

Maestro, this is what I was telling you about? The fingering was like this . . .

> *He plays a few notes on the piano.*

> EVGENIA *has entered with food.*

EVGENIA (*to* KARPOV)

Sh-sh . . . Upstairs . . .

VLADIMIR (*whispers*)

We still need a fourth. Nicky—?

NICKY

I hate cards.

VLADIMIR

Maestro?

KOUSSEVITZKY

I'll be your fourth . . .

> NICKY *puts the record on: "Dear Birch-tree" and plays it softly—mostly for himself.*

> BOHLEN *and* IGOR *enter from the porch, carrying their drinks; moving into here.* IGOR *is in the middle of telling him a story:*

IGOR (*entering*)

He's in Florence. Kolya told me this. I'm telling him about when George was in Florence.

CHIP (*to* NICKY)

A "George" story.

VERA

(*she's got her embroidery out again*) Sh-sh. I think Maria is also sleeping . . .

IGOR (*quietly*)

Of course George knows no Italian. He doesn't even try.

> VLADIMIR *is shuffling the cards, and will soon start to deal.*

CHIP

Here you are, Nicky. We were wondering where you were.

IGOR

So they're in a restaurant and he wants a glass of milk. So George gets on all fours . . .

IGOR gets on his knees.

VERA

Igor . . .

IGOR

—makes a stupid face—and some heart-rending moos.

IGOR moos.

They are laughing.

VERA *(laughing)*

Igor, get up!

They all laugh.

EVGENIA *(to them)*

It's a George story.

IGOR

So the waiter smiles, snaps his fingers—nods a bunch of times, and a few minutes later, triumphantly, he brings George—a large beefsteak!

They laugh.

NATASHA & LUCIA

Sh-sh . . .

*As they quiet down and settle themselves here . . .
the record plays.*

Lights fade.

Scene Five

The same. Later that night; around 2 AM.

The sound of quiet conversations coming from the porch.

LUCIA *is now at the desk, going over accounts, as she can't sleep.*

NICKY *enters, startling her. He still has a drink with him.*

> NICKY

I'm sorry. I was going to use the piano. I didn't mean to bother you.

> *He starts to go.*

> LUCIA

There you are, Nika. We'd all thought you'd gone to bed.

> NICKY

I took a walk.

> LUCIA

Ah.

> NICKY

I sat on the side of some hill. Listened to the trees . . . It's beautiful here. It'll be hard to go back to the city.

> *Sits at the piano.*

> *Plays a note.*

I think I got inspired. By what I heard and saw this evening. Igor and George's dance. But it is the middle of the night.

> LUCIA

Your American was asking where you were.

> *She starts to pick up.*

I'll get out of your way.

> NICKY

No. You don't have to. I don't mind having company. It doesn't bother me. I'm not one of those . . .

> *She looks at the accounts.*

LUCIA (*half to herself*)

Those what?

NICKY

Artists who . . .

He plays a few notes. Stops.
Pause.

I guess I have not been inspired—enough.

Smiles.

And besides I could never write once I'd had a drink. You need a
very clear mind. All your strength. In the morning . . .

LUCIA (*over her books*)

When you're fresh. So— you're quitting?

NICKY

What do you mean by that?

LUCIA

You're not going to—compose. Tonight.

A bit of laughter from the porch.

LUCIA (*continues*)

Igor and your American friend are still out there. Koussevitzky's
gone to bed.

Writing in the account books.

And Vladimir—he doesn't sleep his wife says. I guess he worries
about things.

She looks at him. Then she puts down her pen and
closes the books.

LUCIA

Could I have a sip of your drink?

NICKY

I can make you—?

LUCIA

Just a sip.

He gets up and hands her his drink.

NICKY

I've had enough. Too much. Now I can't work . . .

Smiles.

LUCIA (*as she sips*)
They're going fishing tomorrow morning.

NICKY
Who?

LUCIA
Your American.

NICKY
He's not my—.

LUCIA
And Igor. Maybe others?
Shrugs.
They were asking about poles. What does he want? Does he want something? You must know.
He doesn't respond.
I watched you—in the barn, after he arrived. I'm sorry he came too. This is our house. Koussevitzky knows better.
Then:
Thank you, for all you do. What would we all do without Nicky?
She tries to hand him back his drink.

NICKY
You can finish the rest.

LUCIA
Then I'll go to bed . . .
Sips, then:
He tells such funny stories. George. I don't have to tell you . . .
Then:
He told me one just the other day that I hadn't heard.

NICKY
Everyone has a George story.

LUCIA (*her story*)
This was in the thirties, in Paris—. George had this little sports car— lime green. He loved it. Drove it to England, but coming back he didn't have enough money for the import duty on the car. What could he do? He just gave it to the first person who walked by. That's just like George.

NICKY

It is.

LUCIA

Easy come, easy go. The "artist." They do need to be protected, don't they?

NICKY (*smiles*)

I think we do.

LUCIA (*continues*)

But when he got back to Paris and told—his then wife—she was furious with him.

  Then:

Because, Nicky, this silly woman had just bought a new wardrobe—hat, shoes, purse, dress—all lime green to match the car!

  Laughs.

  NATALIA *comes in.*

NATALIA

The kitchen's clean. Evgenia's made a fruit salad for breakfast.

LUCIA

(*reaches out for* NATALIA's *hand*) My talented dear friend. Who really runs the school of George. She just doesn't get the credit.

NATALIA

Evgenia runs the school. I help her.

LUCIA

That's not what I hear. (*about the kitchen*) Did Anna help?

NATALIA

No.

LUCIA

Where is Anna?

NATALIA

I think I saw her on her way to the barn. But that was some time ago. Should I find her?

LUCIA

No. No. You two have done enough—now go to bed. I'll be up soon too. (*to* NICKY) We're sharing a room—like school girls. (*smiles*)

  NATALIA *doesn't leave;* LUCIA *looks at her.*

NATALIA

George's wife, she was asking if I had seen him.

LUCIA

Tell her he's out on the porch with Igor, they're still working.

NATALIA

She said she'd looked on the porch.

LUCIA

Where is she?

NATALIA

I think she was just going to go back to her room.

LUCIA *nods, shrugs.*

Should I turn lights out? Blow out the candles?

LUCIA

Leave them on. Let them burn. So Anna can find her way home.

NATALIA

Goodnight. Goodnight, Nicky.

NICKY

Goodnight.

LUCIA

I'll be right up.

NATALIA *goes.*
Sounds from the quiet conversation on the porch.

We're like his nuns, Nicky. But none of them understands him like I do. He keeps everything inside. Lets the world see nothing—of his pain. Only me. Only I see this. And sometimes that just feels cruel.

She shrugs, then:

George asked me to ask you . . . A few years ago. Do you know about this?—George—. There was a young dancer. Holly? And there'd been—. She was going to have a child. And George, he helped her— so she wouldn't. Paid for this. There was a witness.

She looks at NICKY.

Some men came to see him . . .

NICKY

Immigration?

LUCIA *(surprised)*

He's an American citizen. You know about this?

NICKY

An educated guess.

LUCIA

What do they want?

NICKY

I don't know. I don't know. *They* probably don't know. It's a good thing, they think, to have. To know. To keep in some drawer. In case . . .

LUCIA

To keep us scared?

NICKY (*shrugs*)

I don't know. In case of—something. What do I know, Lucia? I'm a composer, and I can help buy a goddamn curtain . . .

Looks at her.

I don't know.

LUCIA

I should go to bed—on second thought maybe the porch, and be "hostess."

Smiles.

Goodnight.

NICKY

As she is leaving:

Could you ask Mr. Bohlen to come in here, please? I wish to speak with him for a minute.

LUCIA *is gone.*

NICKY *plucks at the keys. Off we hear* LUCIA *joining the men on the porch.*

After a moment, CHIP BOHLEN *comes in, smiling at* NICKY.

BOHLEN

I thought you went to bed, Nicky? What?

NICKY

Drink?

BOHLEN

I've had enough.

NICKY

I remember what you once told me.

BOHLEN

What?

NICKY

You made a joke. How at the embassy in Moscow, there were two "famous last words." "Alcohol doesn't affect me." And—

BOHLEN

I'm talking with Igor.

NICKY

"And—I understand the Russians."
Smiles.
Very funny. Sit down.
He doesn't.
On my walk. I just took a long walk.
CHIP *looks off.*
I need to talk to you, Chip.
CHIP *looks at him.*
On my walk, I stopped at a stream. And for the life of me I thought I could hear a Jewish band . . . (*explains*) From when I was a child. Accordion, zither, guitar. I thought I could hear one of those plays my family would put on . . . During summer evenings, at sunset. On the lawn. (*then*) I know it was just the sounds of the stream, but . . . This weekend . . . You don't understand.
     Tries again:
I was terribly moved by the work we saw tonight. In that barn. It's been a magical night. I'm sure it must have been for you too. A special night. Probably reminds you of why you're doing what you're doing. Why helping these people is so important.
     Then:
For me though, it was something even more. I wanted to explain.
     Then:
You get away from making art for a while—and I have been very remiss, I haven't written as much music as I should have these past few years.

BOHLEN

You've been doing other things, Nicky.

NICKY (*continuing*)

Tonight I felt—and this is hard for someone who's not an artist to understand what I mean—but I felt—like I belonged in that room today. In that barn in the woods . . . with those great gentlemen . . .

BOHLEN

I'm sure you—

NICKY

Shut up.

BOHLEN *is taken aback and sits down.*

Sorry. But I do need you to be quiet. And not interrupt. And to listen. (then) I felt like I had a home. You probably can't understand . . . How could you? But let me try.

Then:

It was the closest thing to a feeling of—of belonging somewhere, anywhere—that I've felt for a very long time. It's what I now think I've been missing. What I've almost let—get away.

Then:

I know that I've been able to help my friends, my colleagues—I know I've done them good. So it all hasn't been a waste . . .

Short pause.

BOHLEN

May I speak? (NICKY *nods*) But now you think you've done enough.

NICKY

I'm glad you understand.

Then:

<u>Do you want to talk in English?</u>

BOHLEN

Why would I want to do that, Nicky?

NICKY (*continues*)

I need to go back to just being what I was.

BOHLEN

And what was that?

NICKY

An artist. It's as simple as that. I can't say it any simpler. It's what I've learned about myself. Tonight. So . . . (*smiles, reaches into his pocket*) you can have your cards back.

BOHLEN

How will you live, Nika?

NICKY (*smiles*)

Maybe it's time someone helped me.

Waits for BOHLEN *to say something, then:*

I worked for Diaghilev.

BOHLEN *looks at him.*

My music has been played by major orchestras.

BOHLEN

When was the last time?

NICKY (*taken aback, then*)

I could ask Maestro Koussevitzky for a commission.

BOHLEN

Ask him.

He stands.

Excuse me now, I was having a very good talk with Igor. I should go
back to him. He's agreed to be listed as a sponsor for your speech
next month. I've achieved that tonight. I've gotten that.

Laughter from the porch.

NICKY *stares at* BOHLEN.

(*about the laughter*) They're entertaining him. Good.

NICKY (*smiling*)

What speech? You're asking me to give another speech? Do you
understand at all what I've just been—?

BOHLEN

And this one we thought should be on what the Soviets have to done
to—"traditional" Russian culture. And say—how that tradition is alive
only in America today. And with Igor's name . . .

NICKY

Have you heard what I just—?

BOHLEN (*over this*)

I asked George if he'd lend his name . . .

NICKY

What did George say?

BOHLEN

He pretended like he didn't hear me.

Laughs.

He plays his cards close to the vest. He's clever. And cold. He's Georgian. Like Stalin. Maybe you can ask him.

NICKY

He's not like Stalin. Chip, these men are great artists.

BOHLEN (*shouts*)

Just what the hell does that mean?!

NICKY *is taken aback, stunned by this outburst.*

Outside they have heard this too. Silence.

Or why the fuck does that matter?

Then:

And don't ever ever tell me to shut up.

Then:

I don't know why you defend them, Nicky. Would they spend one ounce of sweat defending you?

NICKY

I think they would. (*smiles*) I think they would, and that's where we're so different. You and I. Why we see things so differently. Of course, we come from different worlds. Why *I'm* doing this? Why I'm helping them? It is just to help them, Chip and they know that. And they appreciate that.

BOHLEN (*over this*)

You think we're so different?

NICKY

We are! (*then*) We are. We certainly are. Goodnight.

BOHLEN *looks at* NICKY, *sips his drink.*

BOHLEN

I told myself I wasn't going to tell you, but . . . Why not? Why not? Sitting outside a little while ago. I don't know where you were.

NICKY

I took a walk . . .

BOHLEN

You were on your walk. And your name came up and someone— maybe one of George's harpies, called you a "composer." And Koussevitzky just started to laugh. Why are you laughing, Serge, I ask. "Nicky," he says, "hasn't written a note worth playing for twenty

years. My dog is more of a composer than Nicky Nabokov." He'd
had a few drinks.

    Then:

I played dumb and asked him "innocently" what do you mean,
Serge? "Nikolai Dimitrievich," he said, "is like one of those whores
who have a heart of gold. They come when you call, and they'll let
you fuck them for nothing."

    Then:

All your "friends," they laughed, Nicky. They laughed their fucking
heads off.

    Short pause.

You don't believe me. I should be outside. I was in the middle of
talking with Igor. He's an important man. (smiles) Their fucking
heads off.

NICKY (quietly)

Who was there when he said this? When Koussevitzky said that
about me.

    Then:

Was Igor there?

BOHLEN

Oh he laughed a lot.

NICKY

George?

BOHLEN

A smile. Inscrutable. Stalin . . .

NICKY

Natasha?

BOHLEN

The old wife? She almost fell out of her chair.

    He is gone.

    Laughter from the porch.

    NICKY *is alone. He sits at the piano plays a couple of*
    notes.

    VLADIMIR *peeks in, glass in hand.*

VLADIMIR (big smile)

"You going to die, mister!"

NICKY *looks up.*

That was my Russian. (*smiles*)

    NICKY *closes the piano lid.*

VLADIMIR

Done for the night?

NICKY

Why don't you just take a bottle.

    VLADIMIR *comes into the room, and sets his glass down on "the bar."*

VLADIMIR

I'm going to bed. Are you all right?

    No response.

(*smiles*) Goodnight.

    Starts to go.

NICKY (*stopping him*)

Did you laugh too? At just the idea of my still being a composer?

VLADIMIR

He shouldn't be here. (*then*) We all want to please him. That's what happens when someone like this is allowed here. We say things we think will please him. I'm sorry.

    He sits.

He shouldn't have told you that.

NICKY

Let me be alone, Vladimir.

    Conversations on the porch.

VLADIMIR

Sometimes I think—we hate ourselves. How else to explain—to justify—how we try and please . . .

    Then:

Can I tell you something? (*no response*) When my "Chip" came to me.

NICKY (*looks at him*)

What?? What are you talking about?

VLADIMIR

His name wasn't "Chip." Mine was "Bob." I'd already given up so much. My language. My skill with my language. My art with my language. (*smiles*) This is funny. When I just played in *Crime and Punishment* I thought at least I can use my real accent. I'm playing a Russian! But they said I stood out. I need a Russian accent more like Mr. Gielgud's. An Englishman's Russian accent. It's come to that. It's all as unreal as that.

    Then:

And the director was Russian . . .

    Then:

Your Chip should not have said that to you. I'm sure he now regrets it.

NICKY

Are you speaking for Chip?

VLADIMIR (*over this*)

But now you must forget it. Swallow it. Or spit it out, Nicky.

    Laughter from the porch.

So my "Bob" visited me. By the way I refused a job, so I don't have "cards," I told them no, but none of that matters to them. You're here—you can't say no. You're scared. (*then*) He said, "Vladimir, do you know how the world sees us?"

NICKY

Us?

VLADIMIR (*obviously*)

We—Americans. He had made me an American. Without even asking . . . (then) They see us, "Vlad," as hillbillies. Who beat up on Negroes, and chew gum, and drive big stupid cars. To the world, we Americans are just crude crass idiots who wouldn't know a violin bow from a stick up our ass. Oh, he said, we know they're wrong. So—we need to work to let the world know that they're wrong, about us, Vlad. We need to show them the real us. Our art. And music. And theater. So we need the help of people like you, Vlad. Of artists. Especially you artists who have chosen to leave your god awful stinking country and become one of us here. What a great example you are, for showing the world what we really are like, this country, how generous, and how—free. Would you mind being that example, Vlad? (*then*) It won't cost you anything—if you agree.

    Short pause.

"Vlad," Bob said, "did you know the Soviets have opened their 'House of Culture' in East Berlin? I've seen the pictures," Bob said.

"And boy it's—beautiful. Nice chairs. Marble tabletops. Handsome carpets. Fresh paint and chandeliers. And us—in West Berlin—a goddamn 'information center' that's a fucking hole in the wall, closed half the time, because they don't have the coal to even heat it. That's what we're presenting to the world. That's going to change, Vlad. People like you are going to change that. We'll win this son of a bitch war. We'll show 'em who's got fucking art!"

Then:

What "war" I asked. What war are we fighting now?

NICKY *smiles.*

What?

NICKY

I asked that too. I asked "Chip" that too.

VLADIMIR

And I'm sure Chip laughed just like Bob laughed at me . . . And put his big fucking arm around me and said, "Vlad, that's a good one. That's real funny."

Short pause.

I was headed for bed.

Then:

(*American accent*) "You going to die, mister." My American. That always makes them laugh on the set. I play the fool and make them laugh. What's not to like about such a life?

Lights fade.

Scene Six

The same. Around 5 AM, before dawn.
IGOR and GEORGE sit, drinking. Taneyev's Dawn is
playing on the gramophone.
NICKY stands in the doorway, unseen at first, then:

NICKY

I heard the music. I couldn't sleep. Do you mind?
> *IGOR shakes his head.*
> *They listen until the record finishes. It clicks off.*

IGOR (*to* GEORGE)

Did I ever tell you I met Taneyev?

GEORGE

I think you did.

IGOR (*continuing*)

He had us students all to a dinner. He'd lived with the Tolstoys for
years. He knew Turgenev. A great friend of Tchaikovsky. He'd
known Chekhov. He knew a lot of people. He wasn't a very good
composer though.

NICKY

No? That must have been hard on him.
> *They look at NICKY.*
Knowing so many talented people.

IGOR

That piece is nice though.
> *To* GEORGE.
He taught counterpoint.

NICKY

I sang that in chorus in school. I think I told you that before.

IGOR

Did you? I don't remember.

To GEORGE, *about Taneyev:*
He taught Scriabin. Rachmaninoff.

> NICKY *starts to go.*

Stay.

> GEORGE *looks out the window.*

NICKY

Who's out there? Who's still up?

GEORGE

Lucia's niece. She can't sleep, she says.

NICKY

Like me . . .

IGOR (*with a bottle*)

Have a drink. Sit. Join us.

NICKY

Has Chip gone to bed?

GEORGE

Yes, Nicky, He has gone to bed. (*to* IGOR, *in English*) <u>Mr. Chip</u> . . .
Smiles.

NICKY

Making fun of Chip behind his back?
> *Then:*

(*smiling*) I do it too.

GEORGE

Are you going to sit down, Nika?

> NICKY *takes a drink from* IGOR.

IGOR (*to* GEORGE)

I didn't tell you—<u>Mr. Chip</u> wants to go fishing tomorrow. So we're
going fishing . . .

GEORGE

I'm not going fishing.

NICKY

I've wanted to tell you both how impressed I was today, by what I saw.
And heard. I have one question, though, Igor. I didn't really understand—the ending. Why do you just cut off the fugue? Why do that?

> IGOR *looks to* GEORGE, *then:*

IGOR

Once Orpheus dies—his song has to stop, Nicky. But his lyre—my harp—keeps playing. So the melody is over—but the accompaniment keeps going.

NICKY

I see.

Then:

I see. I could never have thought of something like that. Not in a million years. It is terribly lonely. Very sad.

IGOR

The point.

Short pause.

NICKY

Nice to see Koussevitzky, isn't it?

IGOR (*eagerly*)

It is. (*to* GEORGE) Remember Serge's wife?

GEORGE *nods.*

In Paris I once heard her scream at one of his assistants—"You dirty Odessa Jew." And he was right there. And Koussevitzky's a Jew. How do you not hear things? How does one ignore . . .?

NICKY

You mean, how does one—just swallow that?

He sips.

Let it just roll off your back?

IGOR

Actually, Nicky, it's Koussevitzky I've wanted to talk to you about. (*to* GEORGE) Do you mind?

GEORGE *shakes his head.*

NICKY

With me? What about him?

IGOR

I was hoping you'd do me a favor. You're always so helpful. Thank you. Everyone is always saying how helpful Nicky is. Aren't they?

GEORGE *nods.*

GEORGE

You've been helpful to me.

IGOR (*then*)

I was wondering if you'd do me the favor of speaking with the
Maestro on my behalf—to see if he might commission—me. It's
hard to ask for this sort of thing oneself. I'm sure you understand
that. I'm sure you're the same way.

NICKY

I probably am.

IGOR

And—if you do ask yourself, you risk getting a much smaller fee.
They think you're desperate.
   He looks to GEORGE *who agrees.*

NICKY

I see. I hadn't realized that. I've learned something.
   Smiles.
But I've heard he's commissioning mostly Americans now.

IGOR

I'm American. Chip Bohlen thought it would be a good idea for you
to ask.
   They look at each other.
   Then to GEORGE:

NICKY

And what do *you* want, George?

IGOR (*taken aback*)

That's a little harsh, Nicky. Do you know who you're talking to?

GEORGE

Igor . . . It's fine.

NICKY

I just want to know how can I help. Help more . . .
   GEORGE *looks to* IGOR, *then:*

IGOR

George has been offered La Scala.

GEORGE

Ballet master.

NICKY

I know.

IGOR

We need to keep him here, Nicky. We need to find a way to keep him here. Kirstein can't do it by himself. That's obvious. He needs help.

NICKY

Don't you want to go to Italy? Don't you like Italy, Igor?

IGOR

What are you talking about?

GEORGE

It's worse than Paris, Nicky.

NICKY

So—I'm guessing now—you'd like me to mention this "dilemma" to someone. Someone who maybe could help out. Maybe someone to help out Kirstein.

IGOR

That's right. (*to* GEORGE) And you didn't want to ask.

IGOR *and* GEORGE *share a look.*

Then:

NICKY

There's something else?

IGOR

Nika? Can someone please have a talk with Kirstein?

NICKY

About—?

IGOR

And get him to be more careful.

GEORGE

He means well, Igor.

IGOR

He just published an essay about George. Comparing him to colonial silver, to Emily Dickinson, for Christ's sake.

NICKY

I'll keep an eye on him.

IGOR

Thank you. It just looks silly. And it makes George look scared.

GEORGE

Thank you, Nicky.

IGOR (*to* NICKY)

Do you ever get tired of hearing people's problems?

GEORGE

Nicky's a good person, Igor. He helps people.

IGOR

What are you writing? I don't think I've asked the whole weekend.

NICKY

You haven't.

GEORGE

He's been talking about setting a poem, Igor. "Pushkin's Return."

NICKY

We read that in school.

GEORGE

Pushkin returns home. And finds his country in a big mess.

IGOR

I'd avoid the political, Nika. Thank god, George avoided that.

NICKY

What do you mean?

GEORGE

When I first got here Kirstein had all those crazy ideas for ballets.

IGOR

"Political" ballets.

GEORGE (*bad "accent"*)

George, give me a "hobo jungle" ballet. An "Uncle Tom's Cabin" ballet . . .

NICKY

How did you get out of doing them? Didn't you owe Lincoln—?

IGOR

George pretended he didn't understand, Nika. Didn't you know that's why George doesn't learn any other language—he's afraid he would have to understand too much.

Smiles.

This piece, what is it? Orchestra? Chamber?

NICKY

I'm thinking chamber. It's practical.

Suddenly the hallway light is switched on, LUCIA *enters, and hurries toward the kitchen and the telephone:*

LUCIA (*to* GEORGE, *as she runs in*)

He needs an ambulance!

IGOR

What??

LUCIA (*to* GEORGE)

Sergey needs an ambulance . . .

*She is off as from upstairs a woman [*VERA*] starts to scream.*

IGOR

That's Vera . . .

He starts to hurry off. Passing NICHOLAS *in his pajamas and bare feet.*

NICHOLAS (*entering*)

Mr. Balanchine—!

IGOR (*running off*)

My god . . .

GEORGE

Jesus Christ—.

NICHOLAS

Mr. Sudeikin.

NICKY

<u>What happened?</u>

NICHOLAS

Mr. Sudeikin is throwing up all over himself! He's throwing up blood.

VERA *upstairs continues to scream as*

Blackout

Scene Seven

The same, the study. Morning.

KOLYA is at the piano; IGOR at his side. GEORGE talks with NICHOLAS, who holds the lyre.

During the following: NICKY and then VLADIMIR enter and stand unseen in the doorway, watching:

GEORGE (*to* NICHOLAS)
<u>Nicholas. At the beginning you are at your wife's grave, yes?</u>

KOLYA plays the opening music.

<u>At your wife's grave. All you have to express grief for all you have lost—is music. All you can do—is dance.</u>

IGOR notices them.

IGOR
They're back, George.

GEORGE
Kolya . . .

KOLYA stops playing.

VLADIMIR
He's resting. Nicky likes the doctor. Natalia is staying with him . . . He has a private room.

GEORGE (*to* KOLYA)
He's resting.

IGOR
That man's like a horse.

KOLYA
I should have stayed at the hospital—.

VLADIMIR
No, Kolya. You weren't helping there. He needs to rest. And Natalia knows what to do.

IGOR

How does he look now?

VLADIMIR

Shaken up. Of course.

IGOR

Bless him.

NICKY

Where's Vera?

IGOR

She's asleep.
No one knows what to say.

IGOR

I'll bet he's already insulted three nurses.
They laugh.

KOLYA

Only three? He's slowing down.
Laughter.

IGOR

I'll bet he'll still want to go fishing.
Laughter.
KOUSSEVITZKY *comes in.*

KOUSSEVITZKY

What's funny?

IGOR

Sergey's better. He wants to come back here.

KOUSSEVITZKY

Thank God. That man has nine lives.

KOLYA

At least nine.

KOUSSEVITZKY

I feel better about leaving now.

NATASHA (*following* KOUSSEVITZKY *in*)

Did you take some food? There's still lots of food. George cooked for
the weekend.

KOUSSEVITZKY

Lucia's packed us a lunch.

IGOR

Why can't you stay and go fishing?

KOUSSEVITZKY

George, I'll come to your opening.

IGOR

It's my opening too.

KOUSSEVITZKY

Nicky? You must visit us in Boston. If not Lenox. And play me your
music. I've always so admired your music. I think we all have.

IGOR

Where's "Chip?"

NICKY

Chip is already in Serge's car.
They all hear this.

IGOR

I thought he had his heart set on going fishing.

VLADIMIR

Nicky likes the doctor.

KOUSSEVITZKY (*to* NICKY)

So you found a good doctor up here. Good for you.

NICKY

I didn't "find" him—.

VLADIMIR (*over this*)

He seems good.

KOUSSEVITZKY

A very good one, I hope. It's what he deserves.

VLADIMIR

That's what we were told.
MARIA *enters, at first unnoticed.*

KOUSSEVITZKY

(*to* IGOR, *answering the earlier question*) I'm taking Bohlen back to
Lenox. He can fish there.
Off the honking of a car.

VLADIMIR
Chip seems to be in a hurry. What's the rush?

LUCIA (*calls from off*)
Taxi's here, George.

MARIA (*to* GEORGE)
That's my taxi.
They all notice MARIA.

NICKY
Is Maria—?

IGOR (*explaining to* NICKY)
Maria's going back.

VLADIMIR (*to* NICHOLAS)
Maria is leaving, Nicholas.

NICHOLAS
She's leaving?

GEORGE (*to* MARIA, *over this*)
Later, Maria, we just all are going to visit Sergey in the hospital. I come home tomorrow.
Then:

MARIA
You'll come home, when you come home.
Smiles.

NICHOLAS
Maria, you're leaving?

GEORGE (*to* NICHOLAS)
She wants to go home.

LUCIA (*entering*)
A taxi's here.

GEORGE (*to* MARIA)
Igor and I are getting a lot of work done.

MARIA
I'm sure you are. Would you take this—to the taxi, George?
He takes her bag and heads out.
(*to everyone in the room*) Goodbye.
She starts to go.

NICKY

<u>*Goodbye, Maria.*</u>

MARIA (*turns back*)

Bye, Nicholas. Now it's just you and the Russians.

MARIA *goes out.*

NICHOLAS

Bye . . .

LUCIA

Mr. Bohlen wants to go.

She goes out.

KOUSSEVITGZKY

I should go. I'm sorry to leave like this—.

IGOR

Maybe we should say goodbye? Shouldn't we? To Chip.

IGOR *gets up.*

KOUSSEVITGZKY

I'm sure he'd appreciate that. (*as a goodbye*) Nicky.

KOUSSEVITZKY *and* IGOR *head out.*

NICKY

Maestro . . .

Goodbyes from outside are heard.

NICKY, VLADIMIR, KOLYA *and* NICHOLAS *are alone.*

KOLYA (*plays a few notes, to* VLADIMIR)

The "maestro" hates being around sick people. I heard him say this in the kitchen.

NATASHA (*entering*)

Vera's coming down.

EVGENIA *stands in the doorway.*

EVGENIA (*to* NATASHA)

Do you think I could call long distance? Mr. Kirstein would want to know about Mr. Sudeikin.

NATASHA

I didn't know Lincoln even liked Sergey.

EVGENIA

I'm sure he'd want to know. Maybe send flowers to the hospital.

NATASHA

Call long distance. Lucia won't care.

EVGENIA *goes.*

She can't wait to tell Kirstein everything.

To NICKY *and* VLADIMIR.

She's his spy.

VLADIMIR

Is she?

NATASHA

Haven't you noticed how we're careful what we say around her?

LUCIA (*entering from outside*)

I just asked George what he thought of my niece—as a dancer? He said she wasn't very good—or rather wouldn't be. And would I tell her.

NATASHA

So tell her.

ANNA *has come in with a tray of cups and coffee and a plate of cookies. She is happy.*

(*seeing* ANNA) We all have to grow up. (*to* ANNA) Tired? You look tired.

ANNA

Evgenia assigned me the coffee.

LUCIA *and* NATASHA *help set up the coffee tray. And soon begin handing out coffee.*

VLADIMIR

Maybe we should just get out the samovar. Lucia must own a samovar.

LUCIA

I should.

As IGOR *enters:*

NATASHA (*to* IGOR)

Vera's awake. She's coming down.

IGOR (*taking the coffee*)

Did she get some sleep?

NATASHA

She did.

GEORGE *has entered behind* IGOR.

GEORGE (*to* NATASHA *and* LUCIA)
Maria's off in the taxi. I don't know if she'll catch the train.

NATASHA
Then she'll take the next one.

ANNA
I hope Miss Tallchief makes the train.

LUCIA
We'll set out food in the dining room.

NATASHA
Lucia, no one's hungry.

LUCIA
Just in case . . . Vera's up.

VLADIMIR
(*to the confused* ANNA, *about the coffee*) I'll take that, dear.

IGOR
Should I . . .? (*to the women*) What should I do?
No one knows what to do. They sip their coffee.
KARPOV *appears in the doorway.*
He walks across the floor to ANNA *and the coffee—and his shoes squeak with every step. Everyone notices this.*

KARPOV
What??

GEORGE (*to* IGOR, *about the squeaking*)
Igor, which play—?

IGOR
Cherry Orchard. Yephikhodov, the clerk.

KARPOV
What? (*to* ANNA) Could I have coffee? Four sugars.

NICKY (*as if this proves his point*)
Natasha . . .
NATASHA *takes the spoon from* ANNA.

NATASHA
I'll do it, Anna. He's mine . . . Good morning . . .

She kisses him on the cheek, making the best of this in front of NICKY, *then finishes putting the sugar in his coffee.*

VLADIMIR (*new subject*)
You could tell at the hospital—people were uncomfortable with us.

NATASHA
What do you mean?

VLADIMIR (*kidding* KOLYA)
Kolya wanting to climb into bed with his Uncle.

IGOR
Did you?

NATASHA
You didn't, Kolya?

VLADIMIR
And all his crying? The nurses didn't know what to do with him. Maybe Gielgud was right, and Americans don't like to watch Russians beating their breasts.
　　Laughter.

Their attention turns to the doorway, where LISA *is now helping a very pale and shaken* VERA *into the room. Others stand to help, to give up their seat, etc.*

IGOR
Would you like coffee? I'll get it for you . . .

VERA (*to* IGOR)
Thank you, dear.
　　The room is quite crowded: VERA, LISA, GEORGE, IGOR, VLADIMIR, NICKY, NATASHA, LUCIA, ANNA, KARPOV, KOLYA, NICHOLAS.

No one knows what to say.

LISA (*finally to* VLADIMIR)
So—he's going to be fine?
　　No response.

IGOR
We were saying all the nurses must already be angry at him.
　　Smiles. Laughter.
We're guessing he'll still want to go fishing . . .

No one knows what to say.
Then:

> LISA (*to talk about something*)

Has anyone by any chance seen that movie *The Red Shoes*?

> ANNA (*too much enthusiasm*)

Oh I loved that movie!

> LUCIA

Anna . . .

> KARPOV (*sipping his coffee*)

What's—?

> LUCIA

It just came out, Aleksi. Take Natasha. I haven't seen it yet.

> GEORGE

Maria and I saw it.
> *Then:*

> IGOR

And?

> GEORGE

I thought it—ridiculous. The impresario should be happy if the ballerina and the musician fall in love. What could be better? You have him and her in the same company. It's ideal, the best situation. He's there. She's there.
> *Then as an afterthought:*

Diaghilev would have been very happy with such a situation . . .
> *Others agree.*

> VERA

It's very warm upstairs.
> *Everyone quiets down.*

> NATASHA

What did she say?

> IGOR

It's warm upstairs.

> VERA

I couldn't sleep . . .

> IGOR

Did you open the window?

LUCIA

The windows are open.

No one knows what to say.

NATASHA (*standing, going to the coffee*)

There are cookies . . .

KARPOV

(*hand raised for a cookie, to say something*) Vladimir, what are you on to next?

LISA (*answering for him*)

We're going home.

VLADIMIR

Back to Hollywood.

NATASHA *passes around the cookies.*

LISA

He has a movie.

then:

With Dick Powell.

VLADIMIR

I play Commissioner Luin Chi-Chow. (*his "Chinese"*) "You are going to die—mister." I know the lines.

He smiles. Others laugh lightly as a release. EVGENIA *comes in. Before she can say anything:*

NATASHA (*to* VERA)

Evgenia was saying Lincoln might send flowers to the hospital.

VERA

That would be nice. Sergey always liked flowers. He painted a rose on the knee . . .

GEORGE

He told us.

VERA (*not hearing him*)

—of his Salome . . .

Then:

EVGENIA (*to say something*)

Mr. Kirstein wasn't in.

NATASHA

Keep trying. We really want him to know everything.

EVGENIA (*to* VERA)

I think Mr. Sudeikin might have been even smiling when they took him out in the stretcher.

VERA (*surprised and confused*)

Was he? I didn't notice. I was holding his hand.

LUCIA

I didn't see that. But if Evgenia says—.

EVGENIA

I think he was. I think so . . . (*to* VERA) I wouldn't say if it wasn't true . . .

> *Short pause.*
> *Then:*

GEORGE

He's probably telling the nurses all his stories right now.

IGOR

They won't have the faintest idea what he's talking about.

> *Laughter.*

VERA (*to herself*)

No. No, they won't.

EVGENIA (*to say something*)

Natalia was telling me last night how much Anna wants to be a dancer.

ANNA (*beaming*)

I do. I do.

EVGENIA

George, maybe—another student for our school.

> *She smiles as does* ANNA.
> *Then:*

GEORGE

I don't know.

ANNA

What? (*then*) What do you mean?

> VERA *has begun to talk about* SUDEIKIN, *though at first no one quite knows what she is talking about.*

VERA

We met—during a production of *The Marriage of Figaro*.

GEORGE

Your Aunt Lucia will talk to you about it.

ANNA *is confused.*

VERA

The play not the . . . Not the opera.

ANNA (*to* GEORGE)

What? About what? I don't understand. (*to* LUCIA) What does he mean?

LUCIA

Shhhh—. Later. Shhh . . .

ANNA

But—.

LUCIA

Shhhhh . . .

VERA

I was just hanging around the theater, watching them rehearse . . .

NATASHA (*to others*)

She's talking about Sergey . . .

VERA

I am. He fell in love with me. And he insisted that I be given a part. I'd never acted.

She laughs to herself.

I'd no experience. "I'm not an actress," I said. They created a Spanish dance for me. He designed my costume and decorated it with tiny stars. He started writing me little notes, and signing them—"Figaro."

She smiles at the others.

Wipes her eyes.

IGOR *holds her hand. Big sigh. She turns to* ANNA.

How old are you?

ANNA

Nineteen.

VERA

That's how old I was. And that's how old you were when you left, isn't it, George?

GEORGE

About.

Then:

EVGENIA

I was nine.

NATASHA

I was eleven.

KARPOV

Fifteen.

LISA

Seventeen.

LUCIA

Ten years old.

VERA

We were children. Children leaving home.
　　They sip their coffee, eat their cookies, then:

NICKY

Vladimir and I and found something.
　　He takes out the folded up piece of paper.
It was in the pocket of Sergey's robe.

NICHOLAS. *(seeing the paper)*

Mr. Sudeikin was reading that to me last night when he got ill.

VLADIMIR

In Russian?

NICHOLAS

Yes . . .
　　NICHOLAS *nods.*

NICKY *(reading)*

"I have found myself—at the end of life—poor, living in what I can only
describe as a very ugly room. The smells from the hallway strangle. The
shouts of my neighbors scratch at my face."

VLADIMIR

We think it's—Sergey's speech for tomorrow—*(corrects himself)*
tonight. His name day speech, Vera. What he'd planned for his big
dinner tonight.

NICKY *(continues to read)*

"There are bedbugs. I—who surrounded myself with beauty. I who
loved beauty, and perhaps even created some myself . . ." Bedbugs . . .
　　He looks up.
"It is from this hellish forgotten island, that I speak to you now. To
tell you, my friends, all I have learned and all I know.

Then:

"Strip away everything else from a person, and art is what you have left. Some people call this the soul. But I know it as art. Art: our record that we have lived, the breath that gives us life. They can take away our homes and countries, our families, take away our money and beliefs and hopes; Make us compromise and turn us into creatures we do not recognize. Creatures we might even despise. They can do all that—and then what is left of us—is art. There to remind us that we are human beings. It is not some supernatural gift of the gods, but the most human of human acts. Like eating, like sex, or love, like laughter, like the warmth one feels for family and friends. It is who and what we all are. And it is how we know about ourselves. That's all clear to me now—like never before, dear friends, now that I have been relieved of all the rest . . ."

Short pause.

LISA

We'll all have to act surprised—when he gives that speech tonight.

Laughter/relief.

NATASHA (*to* VERA)

We should eat a little bit. You should, Vera. And then we'll all drive to the hospital.

Then:

Let's go outside. Out on the porch. It's so beautiful out there. Not so stuffy. We can bring food out there. Anna, bring the food out there.

LUCIA (*prodding her*)

Anna . . . (*whispers to* ANNA) We'll talk . . .

ANNA *goes off.*

VERA (*then*)

He scared me . . . But he's going to be fine, isn't he? That's what someone was telling me.

LISA

The nurses are already angry at him, Vera . . . (*to* VLADIMIR) Aren't they? (*to* LUCIA) Help me get her up.

LUCIA *and* LISA *help* VERA *to stand.*

(*to* VERA, *helping her up*) And he wants to go fishing . . .

Everyone starts to stand.

GEORGE (*realizing, smiling*)

So last night—Sergey read that to the boy—in Russian!

Laughter.

VERA

He always needs an audience. I guess it doesn't matter if they can understand or not.

On their way out:

EVGENIA

Everyone's going to come to the hospital?

They nod. Say "Yes." "Of course." Etc.

VERA

He'll like that. He likes attention.

EVGENIA

I'll pack a lunch . . .

She goes.

NATASHA (*to* VERA)

He certainly likes attention . . .

VLADIMIR (*noticing* NICHOLAS)

<u>*Nicholas? Did you understand any of this?*</u>

NICHOLAS

No. I didn't. Nothing.

Laughter.

KARPOV

I guess we're all going to the hospital. And Evgenia's packing us a lunch.

VLADIMIR (*to* KARPOV)

And there will be food on the porch . . .

LISA (*off*)

It's a nice country morning out here . . .

They are gone; short pause.

IGOR, GEORGE, NICKY, KOLYA *and* NICHOLAS *are left.*

GEORGE (*to* IGOR)

Do you want to work?

NICKY (*standing*)

I'll get out of your way—.

GEORGE

You can stay, Nicky.

NICKY *will "drift over" to* GEORGE *and* IGOR.

IGOR

This is so hard on Vera . . .

GEORGE (*to* IGOR)

When we get back to New York, I want to show you the Furies. I'm not happy with that. My work. Tell me what you think.

IGOR

I will.

GEORGE (*smiles*)

I know you will. Sergey once said to me—his speech reminded me of this. It was a good speech.

IGOR

It was.

GEORGE

He said, "George, all I am is a painter. I don't know myself—except as a painter. You can ask a horse why he's a horse, but he just lives a horse's life."

IGOR *and* GEORGE *laugh.*

IGOR (*laughing*)

That's very Sudeikin.

NICKY

It is.

GEORGE (*notices*)

Nicholas, you're still holding the lyre.

He stands.

(to IGOR) And then with that wicked "Sudeikin" smile Sergey said: "But George, perhaps, we'd better not talk too much about it. After all, horses don't talk."

They laugh.

Let's work. Nicholas . . .

NICHOLAS *hurries to him.*

(to NICHOLAS) Orpheus at his wife's grave . . .

He positions NICHOLAS.

(to IGOR) From the beginning?

Places the lyre.

Kolya . . .

KOLYA *plays and just as* NICHOLAS *begins to dance:*

Lights fade.

End of play.

Author's Note

In researching *Nikolai and the Others* I consulted numerous books. I mention a few that were especially important: Nicholas Nabokov's two memoirs, *Bagazh* and *Old Friends and New Music;* Martin Duberman's *The Worlds of Lincoln Kirstein;* Vera Stravinsky and Robert Craft's *Stravinsky In Pictures and Documents;* Stephen Walsh's two volume *Igor Stravinsky: A Creative Spring* and *The Second Exile;* Charles M. Joseph's *Stravinsky & Balanchine;* Bernard Taper's *Balanchine, A Biography;* Richard Buckle's *George Balanchine Ballet Master;* Robert Gottlieb's *George Balanchine The Ballet Maker;* Ballet Society's *Portrait of Mr. B. with an essay by Lincoln Kirstein;* George Balanchine's *Balanchine's New Complete Stories of Great Ballets* (edited by Francis Mason); Francis Mason's *I Remember Balanchine;* Maria Tallchief's *America's Prima Ballerina* (with Larry Kaplan); Vernon Duke's *Passport to Paris;* Arthur Miller's *Timebends*; Carol Gelderman's *Mary McCarthy: A Life*; Jonathan Croall's *Gielgud;* Naima Prevots's *Dance For Export;* and Frances Stonor Saunders's *Who Paid the Piper? The CIA and the Cultural Cold War.*

I also consulted numerous videos of the ballet *Orpheus* as performed over the years by The New York City Ballet, and an extraordinary recording in the New York Library for the Performing Arts, Jerome Robbins Dance Collection, of Maria Tallchief teaching a young dancer the role of Eurydice.

Though based upon research, fact and real people, *Nikolai and the Others* is a play. For reasons of structure and theme I have made some choices that are not factually based: the two largest being—Balanchine first showed Stravinsky his work on *Orpheus* in New York City and not on a farm in Westport. This farm and this weekend are entirely my creation. And Sergey Sudeikin died in 1946, not as suggested in the play, 1948. I have taken other "liberties" as well; the reasons for which I hope are clear. But always my goal has been to present a time and a world as I think it might have been, so that we might experience it, and understand.

—R.N.